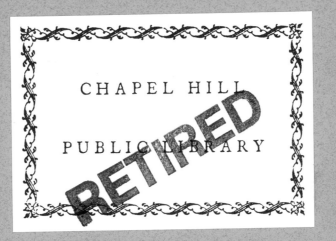

SOUTHERN INTERIORS

SOUTHERN
INTERIORS

Edited by
HELEN C. GRIFFITH

Oxmoor
House®

Library of Congress Catalog Number: 87-62733
ISBN: 0-8487-0740-0
Manufactured in the United States of America

First Edition

Executive Editor: Candace N. Conard
Production Manager: Jerry Higdon
Associate Production Manager: Rick Litton
Art Director: Bob Nance

Southern Interiors

Editor: Rebecca Brennan
Designer: Daniel Hobbs, Creative Services Inc.
Editorial Assistants: Josie Ellixson Lee, Leslie E. Benham
Production Assistant: Theresa L. Beste

Jacket photograph: Colleen Duffley
Jacket photograph, insert: Entrance hall from
A Continental Stance, page 200
Frontispiece: Living room from *For Art's Sake,* page 172

To subscribe to SOUTHERN ACCENTS® magazine, write
to SOUTHERN ACCENTS, P.O. Box 2581, Birmingham,
AL 35202.

CONTENTS

1
THE NEW CLASSICS

2
PERSONAL STYLE

3
INSPIRED BY THE PAST

4
BREAKAWAY PLACES

5
CONNOISSEURS' COLLECTIONS

6
CONTINENTAL TOUCH

7
TIMELESS TRADITION

INTRODUCTION

There was a certain distinctive security to living in a traditional environment . . . within bounds . . . with rules to govern what was acceptable and what was not. An atmosphere of unquestioning complacency, where each segment of the daily routine was compartmentalized in such a way that one rarely blurred into the other. In *The Geography of the Imagination*, essayist and man of letters Guy Davenport describes this sociology of the South in his essay "Finding": "The rule was: everything in its place. To this day I paint in one part of my house, write in another, read in another; read, in fact, in two others: frivolous and delicious reading such as Simenon and Erle Stanley Gardner in one room, scholarship in another." And, for most, that was the way it was before the South became the Sunbelt and ribbons of superhighways connected us to the rest of the states in a very real way. Until recently, young married couples were rarely sent forth to set up housekeeping without the mixed blessing of a few family "pieces" to incorporate into their homes. Granted, a few fortunates were handed priceless antiques. Most, however, were saddled for life with horsehair sofas, a family portrait, and a set of painted china — most often the work of a relative.

Fortunately, the winds of change blew in the opportunity to reevaluate the old mores, especially in the area of interior decoration. Almost overnight, miraculous feats of courage occurred. The inherited dining room table was replaced by chrome and glass, and repro, nondescript chairs gave way to sleek Marcel Breuers. Levolors relieved windows of their heavy damask; parlors became real rooms in which to live;

television was accepted as standard living equipment; and microwave ovens became a way of life.

When we first began gathering information for this book, the inclination was to go along with current trends and present a pictorial definition of Southern style. Much to our delight, we quickly discovered that there is, in fact, no such definitive look. Changing values and life-styles have tilted attitudes toward interiors that represent individual choice — interesting schemes created by real people for real life. Out are prescribed wall colors and window treatments. Gone are hidebound guidelines for proper furniture placement. Finished and dead are stilted flower arrangements. What is "in" is imagination, that all-important ingredient that separates ordinary from extraordinary and unique from commonplace. This book celebrates the most imaginative and diverse of our Southern interiors.

HELEN C. GRIFFITH

SOUTHERN INTERIORS

I

THE NEW CLASSICS

The hallmark of a new classic is an
inventive design concept; a development in the art of
decoration by a tastemaker — by definition,
a tastebreaker — that challenges established customs
by the tendering of creative ideas.
Wrought by enthusiastic leaders and reachers
for new plateaus in the artistic embellishment of
interior space, such compositions are
strictly original. The end result is stylish,
comfortable, and above all,
full of wit.

Dining room from
Design
Metamorphosis,
page 20.

A Measure of Quality

When Dotty Travis was a young girl, she pasted paint and wallpaper samples to the insides of shoe boxes, cut out openings for windows and doors, installed diminutive rug samples, and arranged tiny chairs with covered seats and other doll furniture. Then she stacked the boxes together, and . . . voilà! A house! Dotty's propensity for decorating was obvious; there was never any doubt about what profession she would choose.

FOYER

The sleek appearance of the staircase was achieved by eliminating the traditional pickets and banister, replacing them with a solid, foot-high construction, and adding an elegantly swagged silken rope along the inside wall. A painting of red and yellow flowers by Al Durham hangs above a nineteenth-century French console and accentuates the serene walls with a vivid splash of color.

Otello Guarducci's metal sculpture (right) is displayed against the glazed walls of the dining room, where an acrylic dining table lends emphasis to English Regency chairs and an Aubusson carpet.

As this avowed Francophile searches for fine antiques and innovative decorating approaches for clients, she may find herself poking through a Paris flea market, talking with an antiques dealer in a small French town, or popping off to Düsseldorf on the trail of a piece or two of Biedermeier furniture. She manages to juggle these buying trips abroad with the management of her two Atlanta firms, one an interior design studio and retail antiques shop, the other a wholesale showroom for decorators and clients.

In the course of her career, she has commissioned paintings, invented window treatments, and designed rugs, fabrics, and Lucite furniture. If a piece is missing from a design puzzle, she sorts through her wellspring of ideas until she finds the key. On the flip side, there is as much grit as glamour involved in the business of design. A pair of old shoes tucked in the trunk of her car are used for tramping through muddy jobsites, and she spends as much time reading blueprints and tracking plumbing and electrical outlets as she does toting sample bags in and out of showrooms.

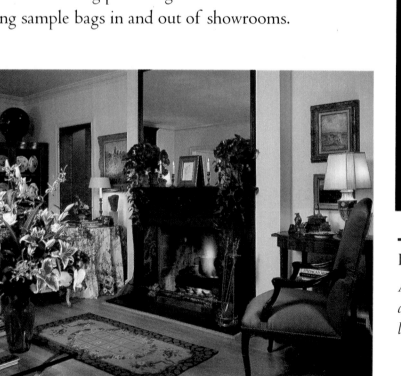

LIVING ROOM

Antique and contemporary pieces coexist comfortably in the warm and inviting living room.

LIVING ROOM

A large-scale painting by Scott Stanley and mirrors on the rear wall fool the eye by appearing to expand the narrow living room. Handpainted pillow fabrics contribute pattern and give life to the subtle, sophisticated palette. An Empire chair stands comfortably in its antiquity against an otherwise contemporary background.

Dotty Travis's design expertise was employed with great effect in her own home. Using it as a laboratory for new ideas, she transformed an ordinary two-story structure into a distinctive address. By installing mirrors, enclosing a side porch, adding trelliswork to a tiny deck, and making other modifications, the house has evolved as a setting full of surprises. Though the floor plan is rather ordinary and the rooms are far from large, the overall effect is one of spaciousness.

During one of the remodeling phases, a garden room was added that wraps around a rear living room window, creating a sunny area overlooking a green garden. This space is not just a room addition, but an integral part of the overall scheme. And because its placement reduced the interior light, the oak floors were stripped and bleached, dramatically shifting the tone of the house from dark to bright.

Since the traditional staircase in the hallway visually absorbed too much space, banisters, handrail, and newel post

DETAIL

A fascinating collection of heads is interestingly displayed on an antique fruitwood commode in the living room.

BREAKFAST ROOM

A grouping of plates painted by artistic frequenters of a Montmartre restaurant is featured in the breakfast room. In typically French fashion, one plate proclaims, "I love brunettes but do not hate blonds."

were replaced by a pared-down white-painted version. Soft gray carpeting complements the stairs' spare lines, and a silken rope looped in graduated levels along the wall serves as a railing. It was structurally unfeasible to enlarge the doorways leading from the hallway to the living and dining rooms, so overpanels were added to lead the eye upward and lend importance to the apertures. The dimensions of the corridor are the same, but these innovative treatments give the hall the generous breathing space it had lacked.

For collectors of all ages, Mrs. Travis's advice is to never settle for second best. With this as her criterion, she has arranged an English Regency chest, a Biedermeier corner cabinet, and a French Empire table — all in the same room: visual proof that mixing periods is not only acceptable but desirable if the quality of each piece can stand on its own. As might be expected, such taste and logic are never out of place.

ENCLOSED PORCH

This tiny enclosed porch is a peaceful retreat for reading, writing, and private moments of contemplation. A terra-cotta sculpture by Amy Podmore adds a lyrical note to the garden, which visually extends the room.

GUEST BEDROOM

A pair of painted iron beds from France is the focal point of the charming guest bedroom. A painting by Al Durham hangs above a fine eighteenth-century French walnut chest.

DESIGN METAMORPHOSIS

People are on the move. And along with a change of address comes the temptation to change life-styles as well. It presents an opportunity to cast out old habits and usher in new ideas.

Few places have enjoyed the influx of people more than Houston, Texas. And few designers have been more influential than Billy Francis in shaping innovative interiors in that city. As a decorator, Francis is keenly aware of the importance of keeping up with trends, being familiar with the marketplace, and directing clients toward items that will withstand the test of time.

His own home is the interpretation of the design he espouses. It is tangible proof that with imagination and determination even a nondescript older home can be transformed into a sleek contemporary without encroaching on the integrity of the neighboring houses.

The house was bought because of its location near the business and cultural center of the city. A bungalow with low ceilings and small rooms, it was the antithesis of everything the designer finds attractive in architecture. But solutions spring from problems, and this house became, for Billy Francis, an intriguing challenge.

LIVING ROOM

The redesign of a nondescript older home provides a distinctive showplace for contemporary style. In the living room, glass windows and doors plus a mirrored fireplace evoke a spacious feeling that is enhanced by the neutral hues of the walls and fabrics. A splash of pattern is provided by a zebra-skin rug placed beneath a glass-and-chrome coffee table. A neon sculpture gives an unexpected splash of color.

In the opening salvo, the house was completely gutted so that the previously fragmented living space could be rearranged and reorganized. At one point, only exterior walls and exposed attic rafters remained to hold the structure together. Most of the attic was appropriated for a vaulted ceiling in the living room, and space was further expanded by opening the walls into a tiny adjoining bedroom to form a study. Former hallways were converted into additional bedrooms and closets.

Then the designer closed the facade of the house to urban Houston by eliminating unnecessary windows. At the same time, by moving the kitchen from the back to the front, he was able to open up the rear with glass windows and doors to embrace the privacy of a fenced backyard. Continuity of design was maintained and further privacy assured by screening the patio, pool, and garden area with the same weathered redwood material used for the home's exterior.

The interior is uncluttered and straightforward. All room

KITCHEN

The kitchen features dove gray plastic laminated cabinets, white countertops, and shiny black Italian ceramic tile. The backsplash beneath the cabinets on the right is actually a window.

STUDY

Forest green wool limousine cloth covers the walls, table, chair cushions, and vertical shades in the study. The neutral accent provided by a Karl Mann collage complements the subtle variations of pattern in the upholstery fabrics and rug.

settings display good furnishings and striking accents against rich, solid background colors. An extra dimension was added to the solid colors by opting for unusual fabrics. In the dining room, walls and ceiling are sheathed with black billiard cloth to form a dramatic setting for a rosewood table paired with Lucite chairs. For his study, Francis chose dark green limousine cloth to cover the walls, sofa, vertical shades, and shelves. Billiard and limousine cloth introduce interesting, and desirable texture to these rooms, and their sound-deadening qualities provide a measure of relief from urban noise.

Remodeling and decorating on such an extensive scale was no small undertaking, but the work moved quickly thanks to careful planning. In five months, the metamorphosis was complete — a modest dwelling had been transformed into a sleek, sophisticated design statement.

BATH

A wall-to-wall mirror, shiny gray walls, and black countertop give this small bathroom a sophisticated appearance. Greenery in a pottery urn and a Chinese basket add visual fillips.

MASTER BEDROOM

Walls covered in vertical linen string cloth and a floor-to-ceiling bed canopy establish a linear motif in the master bedroom. The quiet, neutral colors are an effectively simple background for a distinguished Biedermeier breakfront and bedside tables.

LIGHT & NAUTICAL

The interior designer began planning the decor of this Grove Isle condominium in Coconut Grove, Florida, while the high-rise complex was only a shell of a building.

While construction was still underway, decorator Juan Montoya and his client took exploratory elevator rides up and down the units overlooking Biscayne Bay. Their objective was to select the best floor and location for the condominium the prospective owner planned to buy. In one of the units, they got off on the tenth floor and stood on an unfinished cantilevered terrace. As Montoya looked out over the buildings and bay, he experienced a sensation of sailing into a harbor. He realized then that he had discovered the right location for his client's new home, and the nautical image he conceived shaped the plans for the airy, light-filled interior he was to design.

The Colombian-born decorator had excellent credentials for the assignment. After studying architecture in his native country for two years, he completed his studies at the Parsons School of Design in New York and went on to Paris to begin his practice. There, although he was virtually unknown, a fortuitous turn of fortune's wheel landed him an opportunity to decorate the private apartment of a prominent diplomat. Thus established, he subsequently studied furniture design in Milan and eventually returned to New York to found his own corporation.

LIVING ROOM/DINING AREA

A raised platform separates the living and dining areas but allows the space to read as one. "Boat lights" are built into the platform for a nautical ambience. A variety of textures creates interesting contrast.

BAR

Mirrored doors cleverly conceal a bar in the angled wall in the living room/dining area. Brushed aluminum cabinets add a crisp sheen.

DINING AREA

A dazzling view of Biscayne Bay can be seen from the dining area, where rounded shapes suggest the curved lines of a boat's interior. Montoya selected ash for the bleached and stained table he designed because of the wood's light color and distinctive grain.

The designer made his mark as a minimalist, and although his style has softened over the years, he is still a devotee of clean design. He believes that each element within a room — an entrance, a view, a chair, a piece of art — should be featured individually. Not surprisingly, then, he is skeptical of the opposing trend which he regards as a "renaissance of clutter." He observes that clutter can create distraction and that the designer's primary function is to place objects so that they stand on their own merit.

In the Grove Isle condominium, there is a foyer, dining room/living room area, master bedroom, and two additional bedrooms. Several major alterations were made during construction to customize the interior space. Since the dining area presents a stunning view of the bay and the living area overlooks water as well as land, the dining room floor was raised to separate the functions of the two and permit the dining room an even more spectacular vista. A nearby breakfast area was also elevated, and one of the living room walls was angled and mirrored to reflect the exterior view, which becomes an integral part of the room. Storage space thus created is used for stereo equipment and a bar. A wall between the living room and an existing bedroom was removed to make a sitting room/den. And finally, the rough-surfaced popcorn ceiling throughout was covered and painted with lacquer. The result is a sleek, organized look.

Numerous elements contribute to the nautical motif. First, there is the predominant use of white, the quintessential color associated with boats. When the designer initially inspected the apartment in its raw state, he decided to retain the natural

BREAKFAST AREA

The breakfast area presents an unobstructed view of the bay. The storage wall holds everything from an ironing board to china and crystal.

GUEST BEDROOM

An all-white color scheme gives the guest bedroom a cool, serene look. A deck chair and twin beds upholstered in canvas play up the nautical theme, while nickel-plated fixtures add balance and sculptural elements to the walls. A Bambara tribe urn and bowl rest on the white rattan chest. Vertical and horizontal blinds form an intriguing grid pattern on the window.

concrete color to reinforce the effect of coolness; thus whites and neutrals became a canvas for the reflected colors from outside. The rounded shapes of the furniture in the living room/dining area and den suggest the curved lines of a ship's interior, and "boat lights" built into the dining platform are focused to send shimmers of light across the glazed Italian floor tiles at night.

The airy, open condominium provides a striking setting for entertaining as many as sixteen dinner guests and easily accommodates the owner's growing collection of pre-Columbian artwork. Many of these pieces are displayed in the sitting room/den. A sculpture by Franco Ciarlo commands the foyer, and other works are found in the corridors outside the bedrooms.

Contrary to what might be expected in this pristine interior, maintenance is simple. Heavy polyurethane protects wood surfaces, the floors require a minimum of care, and living room furniture is covered in durable, elegant leather.

Projecting a sense of serenity and order, as would be proper aboard ship, this elegant setting exudes an open invitation to relax, to linger, and to enjoy.

ENTRANCE

A sculpture by Franco Ciarlo at the entrance to this Coconut Grove, Florida, condominium is shown against a portion of the owner's collection of pre-Columbian art in the sitting room/den.

THE HIGH LIFE

Adapting to rapid-fire changes in life-styles is as important in the world of today's top executives as the ability to make sharp business decisions. The chief executive officer of a large chain of department stores approached his relocation from California to Georgia with the philosophy that experiencing life in different parts of the country gives one a truer perspective of what is happening — not just in business, but in the arts, architecture, and the community as well.

He and his wife had, apart or together, lived in Boston, Denver, New York City, and Los Angeles. So they arrived in Atlanta for their first experience with life in the Deep South bringing a collection of contemporary, country, classic, and neoclassic furnishings from their former homes. Having

DINING AREA

An ultrasophisticated contemporary banquette and table in the dining area are contrasted with a pair of Louis XVI opera chairs. Annette Cone Skelton's Torn Paper Series of Seven *hangs along the wall.*

LIVING/DINING LEVEL

The main section of the living and dining level reflects a preference for "compatible contradiction." An ancient Philippine Bontok jar stands behind a contemporary sofa covered in an elephant skin fabric.

always lived in the inner city, with a country house for weekends, they decided to purchase a duplex penthouse condominium in a residential complex and then redesign it to their tastes.

View-restricting walls and partitions were removed, terraces incorporated to expand interior space, hallways abolished, and baths and kitchen magnified. In collaboration with their designer, Dan Carithers, they took the condominium back down to its "architectural bones" in order to create a space for luxurious living and entertaining.

It was a shared enthusiasm for "compatible contradiction" that brought the designer and the homeowners together. The couple had restored a 250-year-old French stone farmhouse in upstate New York and renovated a fifty-year-old Bauhaus home overlooking Los Angeles. The challenge was to blend the furnishings from these divergent homes and the couple's collected art and artifacts into yet a third environment.

And a compatible contradiction it is. Gleaming white oak hardwood floors support a trilevel open-air Bauhaus staircase that appears to float up from the suspended entry into a glassed-in living and dining level. Once there, sliding glass doors open to a stunning panoramic view overlooking the

LIBRARY/GUEST ROOM

In the library/guest room, a two-story glass wall opens to the floor above. The walls are paneled in stainless steel cladding, and floor-to-ceiling adjustable bookshelves are filled with a collection of Southwest American Indian baskets and artifacts. For privacy, sliding glass doors and horizontal blinds separate the room from the adjoining master suite.

SITTING ROOM

Situated between the library and master bedroom, the sitting room not only extends the privacy of both areas, but serves as a guest bedroom as well when closed off by heavy bifold panels.

historic Ansley Park section of midtown Atlanta. The lower floor consists of a convertible library/guest room that adjoins the master suite and spa. In the library, a two-story glass wall opens the space to the living room above and to the city below. Sliding glass doors and horizontal blinds separate the library from the master suite without permanently interrupting the flow of space. The master suite has a built-in custom bed module that economizes on space, while capitalizing on the splendid view. Again, there are sliding glass floor-to-ceiling doors which allow breezes to enter the suite and flow into the spa.

In the spa, white tile walls and floor, a rare St. Laurent black marble-covered vanity, and endless mirrors create a streamlined background for luxurious bathing and dressing. But the pièce de résistance is an eight-foot whirlpool tub.

The condominium, with its urban chic and breathtaking city overlook, is another indication of a rediscovery of inner-city living at its finest. Situated among shops and restaurants, it is close in, convenient, and cosmopolitan.

LIVING/DINING LEVEL

(Overleaf) A Bauhaus staircase leads from an open terrace to the glassed-in living/dining level. On either side of a nineteenth-century French garden table are antique Louis XIV gilt chairs.

KITCHEN

The custom kitchen, which opens to the living area to facilitate service, boasts state-of-the-art appliances. A collection of eighteenth-century American kitchen utensils provides decoration as do the ceramic pears by Paul Nelson.

MASTER SUITE

A built-in bed module economizes on space in the master suite and capitalizes on the view. A handsome Directoire accent table and Regency side chairs grace the window.

2

PERSONAL STYLE

There is not now, nor can there
ever be, a formula for personal style. It is
not a "thing" to be dissected
and analyzed, but a fresh, engaging,
exciting "way." An intangible, it springs naturally
and unselfconsciously from highly
charged imaginations. It is the
singular ability to get the very most out of the
commonplace . . . the
celebration of the familiar seen
from a unique perspective.

Dining room from
Relaxed Elegance,
page 72.

LIVING ROOM

Bleached canvas upholstery provides a subdued background for the owners' varied collection of objets d'art. An Indian dowry box is centered on an acrylic cocktail table, and an inverted Pakistani copper cooking vessel rests on the hearth. Antique ginger jars on the mantel hold roses from the garden.

COMPATIBLE COLLABORATION

The adage "Never judge a book by its cover" could easily apply to the conservative Dutch Colonial home that sits comfortably among other turn-of-the-century houses in the Myers Park section of Charlotte. The unpretentious, predictable exterior betrays no hint of the unexpected delights within.

The traditional framework has provided the owners every opportunity to combine classic and contemporary styles with minimalist restraint. They feel that the strength in the architectural shell of the house affords an ideal surrounding for the kinds of art and furniture that they collect.

Among the features that first attracted the couple to the house were high ceilings, abundant natural light, and the location of the kitchen at the rear center of the house. One of the owners is an artist, so adequate space combined with hours of daylight was essential. However, it was the symmetry of the interior plan coupled with the timeless character of the house that was most impressive.

EXTERIOR

White trim against soft gray clapboard accentuates the clean lines of an eighty-year-old Dutch Colonial home in Charlotte, North Carolina.

The focal point in the entry is a striking sheet metal and brass-trimmed table by John Dickinson. The table serves as an introduction to the home's eclectic interior design concept. Above it hangs a minimalist canvas by Kimberly Kyser. These two spare, sophisticated elements are contrasted by a pair of topiary myrtle trees and an heirloom box topped with a tiny bird's nest. The juxtaposition of such diverse materials in a carefully arranged collage establishes a pattern that will be repeated throughout the house.

Walls, ceilings, and moldings are painted white to produce a unifying neutral background suitable for an intensely personal collection of contemporary art. And although the furnishings are deliberately low-key, the simplicity of line and economy of decor are deceptive. In each room, such unexpected objects as a baroque architectural fragment, an old carved wooden finial, or an antique clock have been strategically placed to puncture the severity of a static image.

Another dramatic surprise attributable to the owners is the

ENTRY

John Dickinson's dramatic sheet metal and brass-trimmed table highlights the entry and establishes the decor. A pair of miniature myrtle trees flank a tortoiseshell box, which is topped by a small brass heirloom box and a bird's nest. Hanging above the table is a minimalist canvas by Atlanta artist Kimberly Kyser.

DINING ROOM

The motif established by the metal table in the entry is repeated in the dining room with a table skirt of gray flannel bordered in white canvas. Two lamps, the bases cast from originals by Diego Giacometti, stand before a painting by Kimberly Kyser. Period chairs covered in leather surround an acrylic-and-glass table.

KITCHEN

The redesigned kitchen features gray green marble counters and open glass shelves. Abundant natural light from the window-wall bathes the area.

functional two-story addition across the rear of the house. On the first level, large window-walls extend across the completely redesigned kitchen, while on the second floor, windows form a new clerestory that floods the artist's studio with light. Especially charming is the two-tiered terrace that leads to the side porch, where French doors, now framed by white columns, open up the once screened-in area.

The contrasting, yet compatible, facade of the house and the counterpoint of objects within reveal the Janus of the owners' artistic interests and creative originality — a forward-seeking eye for things modern with a backward-looking appreciation for the past.

LIVING ROOM

An Italian architectural fragment and an antique French clock blend comfortably with the uncluttered lines of the living room.

EXTERIOR

A series of columns replaced the original porch screens and created a colonnade for the two-tiered terrace at the rear of the house.

KITCHEN

In the kitchen/breakfast area, furnishings and accessories are in a mélange of bright colors. Folk art basketry is combined with a collection of Americana that includes an Early American pine armoire and an old-fashioned penny scale.

An Eclectic Scenario

With its geranium-filled window boxes and ivy-covered stucco walls, a northwest Atlanta home exudes an old-world charm that is allied with contemporary dimensions and large-scale architectural detailing. The effective combination of the stonelike facade and wood-tie steps overlays a sense of tradition on an essentially modern living space. It is this juxtaposition of complementary mediums that gives definition to the uniquely designed interiors.

The homeowners had been long-standing admirers of their interior designer, Penny Goldwasser, who approaches decorating as an artist approaches a blank canvas, but instead of artists' oils, she uses form, color, and texture to create her design image. For the owners, just to be around her was a learning experience that led unconsciously to a new way of thinking about decorating.

The initial impression of the house is one of lessons well learned. With the first step into the foyer, there is an instant awareness of the flow of space and light, of one area blending into another. Throughout the house, furnishings are arranged to create a sense of discovery and contrast, a feeling of different periods working together in harmony.

EXTERIOR

Built on hilly acreage and surrounded by pines and dogwoods, an Atlanta residence combines contemporary dimensions with old-world touches, evidenced by colorful flower-filled window boxes and clinging ivy.

The architectural background is ideally suited for this interplay. Following the owners' dictates, walls are off-white, a neutral backdrop that contributes to the sense of spaciousness. The large, sunny living room, its vaulted ceiling open at one end to a study and master suite above, is proportionally complemented by the relatively small size of the adjacent dining room, and beyond that, a kitchen/garden room. On all sides, sets of French doors lead from living and dining areas to separate sheltered terraces. Window treatments have been eliminated to orient views to the landscape and to let in light.

As quickly as this initial welcoming wash of atmosphere is absorbed, attention is redirected from the outdoor scene by recessed shelves, positioned on either side of the living room windows, that showcase the homeowners' fine assemblage of primitive art and crafts. Separate groupings of early Mediterranean, pre-Columbian, and African pieces attest to the couple's interest in these exuberant art forms.

Important as these collections are, however, they seem only one measure of the owners' highly personal and creative taste. Wherever the eye is apt to rest — whether caught by the classical imagery of a silk obi-covered floor screen or the delicacy of a crocheted shawl draped as a sofa throw — family mementos and treasures are incorporated as imaginative works of art. But for all the rich detail of these individual pieces, the main interest is in their arrangement. A sense of design continuity is achieved through the use of eclectic combinations and contrasting mediums — polished and rough surfaces, sophisticated and handcrafted appointments.

Color is the unifying factor. In the living room, the tone is set by the tawny cream, blue, and mellow peach pattern of the antique Oriental rug, while accents range from browns and

LIVING ROOM

Furnishings from the past are mingled with comfortable seating in the entertainment area. Built-in shelves displaying an assemblage of pre-Columbian pieces are juxtaposed with a black lacquered sewing table from the Orient. An antique English library table, cut down to coffee-table size, provides a handsome base for the stone swan cachepot.

beiges to plums. The dining room uses many of the same colors but intensifies them through the use of a rich floral pattern on slipcovered chairs.

Within this context, the most ordinary and extraordinary objects have been transformed into functional and engaging accessories. Though the decor cannot be defined as having a regional specialization or style, the mood conveyed is one of "countrified" eclecticism executed with restraint. The home's warmth and directness of style seems to emanate from the owners' own personalities.

DINING ROOM

A penchant for irreverent combinations is exemplified by the bare-bones charm of an English schoolboy's pine table laid with fine crystal and china.

FOYER

The herringbone-patterned brick floor in the foyer continues into the dining room. Primitive figures from Africa and Mexico, displayed in built-in cases on each side of the entryway, serve as conversation pieces for arriving guests. Chairs, slipcovered in a bright floral material, enhance the warm, lively atmosphere.

The foyer (right) is furnished with a combination of European and Oriental antiques that includes a silk obi-covered floor screen and an antique Chinese rug.

AT THE WATER'S EDGE

The long drive winding across a carefully manicured lawn edged with magnolias and pines gives no clue to the house that appears suddenly over the last rolling hill. The Memphis, Tennessee, residence nestles comfortably in a natural setting bounded by the waters of Blue Heron Lake, its cypress exterior adding to the illusion that the structure has always existed in the landscape.

Site placement for the house was determined in relation to that of the owners' former home on the same property. The earlier residence, one of the oldest in the county, is on a hill overlooking the lake. But after seventeen years of mowing surrounding acreage, the decision was made to build a smaller, more functional house closer to the water's edge.

GALLERY

In the front gallery, morning sun pours through the wide entry to illuminate the brilliant colors of an antique kilim rug. The gallery connects the kitchen and bedroom areas and also opens directly onto the living room entrance, which is flanked by greenery and twin pianos.

EXTERIOR

The giant white flowers of a Henryi clematis vine climb skyward on the cypress posts supporting the entrance arbor to this Memphis home, which is built in the vernacular style of a Texas ranch house. Terra-cotta bricks selected for the walk blend with the Mexican tiles used throughout the interior.

There was no trouble deciding on an architectural style. A native Texan, one of the owners was drawn to designs found in and around San Antonio that reflect the vernacular of early Texas houses. However, realizing that this regional style would have to be adapted to the Tennessee landscape, a nontraditional approach was chosen, one that exhibits many of the characteristics of timeless western ranch houses. A weathered look, achieved by the choice of gray-stained cypress siding, was enhanced by a stucco chimney and Mexican tile chimney pots. The roof is a metal standing seam design. Across the front entrance, the posts of a cypress wood arbor are covered each spring and summer with large white clematis.

The couple requested a scheme that would include several large rooms conducive to entertaining. To this end, the finished plan features enclosed galleries with oversize double doors at both ends that open up the living space from front to back. The home's private area contains three bedrooms, including a master suite with a sitting room and greenhouse. During spring and summer, breezes blow through every room, and if the air is still, thirteen ceiling fans circle to stir up their own ventilation. Eight skylights combine with the fans to augment the sensation of light and air.

DINING ROOM

Situated in the rear gallery, the dining area opens to the terrace and views of the lake and nearby pool. Framing the scene are white sailcloth draperies bordered in accent colors picked up by the high-gloss lacquer of the dining room chairs and the Portuguese needlepoint rug.

Vibrant colors reminiscent of the southwest run rampant throughout. Rough plaster walls painted a high-gloss white or turkey red provide the appropriate backdrop for coordinating hues and accents of mustard yellow and parrot green. Unglazed Mexican tile floors reinforce the theme. Keyed to an atmosphere of fun and flamboyance, not one but two pianos hold forth in the entrance hall. And in the kitchen/sitting area, palm tree columns, inspired by those found in a favorite room at the Royal Pavilion in Brighton, England, lend an appropriate yet unexpected note of exuberance to an otherwise utilitarian space.

The lake, which attracts many wild waterfowl to its protected shores, is not far away. Just a few feet offshore, a small island is connected to the lawn by a footbridge, where at twilight fish gather for an evening meal and ducks expect a daily ration of corn. In winter when the lake freezes over, friends are invited to skate and sled. They have music to heighten their enjoyment and lights to illuminate their way in a setting where nature has been not just protected but lovingly enriched.

LIVING ROOM

A high ceiling of wide wood planking reinforces the feeling of airy relaxation in the living room. Comfortable seating upholstered in active patterns and vibrant solids provides a lift to the traditional decor. Antiques of note include a wine cooler, serving as an end table, and an eighteenth-century English globe in its stand near the hearth. Built-in bookshelves frame a large oil painting by Edward Giobbi.

KITCHEN

Similar to architectural elements seen at the Royal Pavilion at Brighton, England, palm columns constructed of wood with tin leaves create quite a conversation piece in the kitchen. A collection of works of art and family memorabilia hangs on the far wall. A Victorian-era English duck painting is positioned over the mantel.

MASTER SUITE

Turkey red lacquer walls and a cotton rag area rug in tones of red, pink, and brown add warm color notes in the master suite. The space includes a private sitting area, where a portrait by Charles Inzer hangs over an antique pine mantel salvaged from a Houston convent.

SCREENED PORCH

(Overleaf) Affording ever-changing views of the lake, a large screened porch across the back of the house is a favorite gathering place during the temperate spring and summer months. In keeping with the outdoor ambience, the floor is covered with a sisal rug, and the comfortable willow furniture sports durable white sailcloth cushions.

LIVING ROOM

A painting by Marion McClanahan, flanked by a pair of Staffordshire cats, hangs above the mantel in the living room. An antique French chair is covered in muted watercolor tones. Behind it, a painting by J. A. Rice is displayed above a Country French buffet, and near the doorway to the dining room is a painting by Whittier Arnold Wright.

A MEASURE OF CHOICE

The most intriguing thing about this Atlanta house is that it is "little." Located on a quiet street high above historic Peachtree Creek, the one-story, gray shingled bungalow with the living/dining room and kitchen on one side and two nice bedrooms on the other has great appeal. But it measures a mere 975 square feet.

Though small, the house has a near-perfect floor plan with few interruptions in wall arrangement, as well as attractive moldings, good hardwood floors, adequate closets, and the possibility of adding a large screened porch across the back that would provide the equivalent of an extra room. Perhaps best of all, within these delightful confines, all of the owners' furnishings — French antiques; collections of blue-and-white porcelain, majolica, and tortoiseshell boxes; and a myriad of distinctive accessories — lie within arm's reach. As a further endorsement for smaller houses, the home's owner/designer, who heads her own decorating firm, Candler Lloyd Interiors,

EXTERIOR

Morning sunlight dapples the brick courtyard and gray shingled walls of a cozy bungalow located in a shady north Atlanta residential area.

feels that it is easier to make a small room special because it takes a lesser investment of time and money to fill one up.

Starting with the entrance hall, she seized upon a master stroke by placing an important antique French tall clock against an overscale print wallpaper of blue-and-white plates on a deep salmon background. By itself, the clock fills the space, and the brilliant color and pattern do the rest. The main living area reveals the decorator's preference for intricate motifs and clear, fresh colors. For longevity, she chose good upholstered furniture with classic lines and proportions to which she added such graceful pieces as a Country French buffet and an Indian teak coffee table.

In this little house, the question of size has been laid to rest. Here is proof that with a superior sense of style a little space is quite enough. For these homeowners, at least, big things in little bungalows has a certain proverbial ring.

RELAXED ELEGANCE

Situated in the heart of the city's Garden District, this New Orleans residence is a virtual art gallery where special attention has been lavished on both the fine and decorative arts. With a sophisticated and knowledgeable eye, the owner has assembled a collection of English furniture and paintings, French and Italian drawings and bronzes, and Oriental porcelains. These, together with family portraits and works by well-known Louisiana artists, reveal the fact that this homeowner is a serious collector.

Through his background in law, English literature, and history, and after many years of travel in search of the interesting and unusual, this connoisseur has developed a predilection for the antique, with a special fondness for the

ENTRY

In the entrance hall, a collection of English watercolors flanks a French nineteenth-century trumeau above an eighteenth-century Chippendale table. A French bronze-and-crystal chandelier hangs above an antique Kurd rug.

EXTERIOR

Framed by stately oaks, this Garden District home in New Orleans dates from 1870 and represents a modified Greek Revival style.

LIVING/DINING ROOMS

A large doorway with pocket doors separates the living and dining rooms. English watercolors hang beside an eighteenth-century English secretary, and the portrait above, circa 1760, is of the school of Sir Joshua Reynolds.

Living Room

Nineteenth-century Chinese temple guardian horses are positioned on either side of an eighteenth-century English clock in the living room, and a distinguished collection of European old master drawings covers one entire wall. The upholstery and drapery fabrics were carefully selected to complement the biscuit color of the walls.

LIBRARY

A floral chintz sets the tone for the comfortable downstairs library. Antique English needlepoint pillows and a nineteenth-century English papier-mâché tray table punctuate the seating area defined by an antique Bessarabian rug. A set of botanical prints by Sir Joseph Paxton frame an 1884 painting by Andres Molinary.

English style. On regular trips to England and the Continent, he combines business and pleasure in his quest for the beautiful items that furnish his home and also augment the impressive collection at the prestigious St. Charles Gallery, which he owns.

His true collector's passion is most clearly articulated in the elegantly furnished living room, where a distinguished group of European old master drawings from the fifteenth through the eighteenth centuries is displayed. And although it may be the drawings that receive the most attention, other objets d'art of equal interest are artistically arranged in the room. A small bronze torso by London sculptor Tom Ogle,

POWDER ROOM

The decorative wallpaper chosen for the tiny powder room creates a surprising feeling of spaciousness.

for example, is one of the owner's favorites, as is a signed early eighteenth-century clock with works by Christopher Pinchbeck, the famous English clockmaker and metallurgist who invented the Pinchbeck formula found in antique gold jewelry.

The richly furnished living and dining rooms exhibit a calculated restraint, while an adjacent library, which opens to the patio overlooking the swimming pool, is somewhat less formal. The spaces, orchestrated by interior designer Mary Ferry Bigelow, are visually harmonious, and the openness and easy flow are especially conducive to entertaining.

The variety of decoration, the distinctive collections, and the wealth of interesting detail combine to give this Garden District home a fitting atmosphere of relaxed elegance.

GUEST BEDROOM

A subtle striated wallpaper and delicate floral border coordinate with the fabric used in the draperies and dust ruffle in the guest bedroom. Pillows were made from antique Caucasian rugs, and the large music bench has a seat cover of eighteenth-century needlepoint. Two Japanese folding screens, circa 1880, are mounted above the bed.

RHYTHM & HUES

The three-storied Georgian exterior is austere: a corner town house condominium, part of a row of gray-stuccoed facades, shuttered and drawn against the Mobile sun. But like the drumroll that precedes a gentle orchestral score, such no-nonsense symmetry introduces a seductive rhythm within.

Under the direction of New Orleans designer Tom Collum, the tempo set in motion for the family in residence is repetitive yet subtle; there is a cadence to the decor and a cadence to the watercolor flow of washes and tints that forms its backdrop. Flowers — at times precisely bordered and at others allowed to run riot — drift over chintz-covered furnishings, papered walls, and handpainted rugs.

This arresting and ineffably personal design concept evolved from the long-standing relationship between the designer and the owners. The wife, a former business associate of Collum, had also collaborated with him on the interior design of the couple's previous houses.

ENTRANCE

In the entrance, a mirrored wall visually expands the foyer's dimensions. Reflected in its sparkle, a pair of silk-covered Directoire bergères and a flower-filled vase atop the Louis XV-style console add a blush of color.

GARDEN ROOM

A Louis XV pine wedding armoire, circa 1780, and painted buffet, circa 1760, delineate a comfortable seating area in the garden room. An oil by Mobile artist B. Tucker provides a splash of color.

The couple had returned to their native city after several years' absence. And with two preschoolers, an Old English sheepdog, and a large collection of furnishings in tow, they intended to make the condominium their home for just the time it would take to find property and build a house. Ultimately, the interim stretched into years; the sheepdog departed; another baby arrived. Yet by building upon the accommodating design framework, they discovered their well-laid plans could not have gone awry more beautifully.

At the outset, owners and designer were faced with the straightforward, rather anonymous proportions typical of town houses today. All were in complete agreement that fine-tuning the condominium's existing structural design was the first and best rebuttal to the constraints imposed by such

LIVING ROOM

In the living room, chintz fabric, sprays of roses, Chinese porcelain fruit, and framed botanical engravings by Redouté above the Louis XV-style lit de repos suggest a garden oasis.

LIVING ROOM

Delicate as a pair of fluted lilies in the field, Art Deco glass-topped consoles flank the doorway leading into the dining area. The arrangement of antique French and contemporary furnishings in the living room, underscored by the delicacy of handpainted sisal rugs, issues a gracious invitation for relaxation and conversation.

DINING ROOM

Creating a three-dimensional effect, the floral tracery of handblocked paper covers the walls and ceiling of the dining room. Vases of flowers from the garden, which adorn the Brueton dining table and top the Régence iron-and-marble console, perpetuate the floral theme. A Louis XV-style open-cage chandelier illuminates the table and surrounding Louis XVI-style chairs.

conventional spaces. To this end, hardware and light fixtures were upgraded and replaced, large glass doors were installed in the dining area to reveal an exterior courtyard, and wall mirrors were placed in the downstairs foyer and garden room.

A sleight-of-hand use of color introduced additional excitement. The rectangular living room was given instant character and definition by the application of a soft grayed pink on walls and ceiling. Then in dressing out the adjoining rooms, other grayed values of soft mauves, greens, and blues spin off the floral fabric used on the living room lit de repos. The skilled attention that is paid to the transition of hues from room to room contributes to an element of continuity, while the use of off-white walls with color accents overhead gives the rooms a feeling of infinite space.

GARDEN ROOM

A charming breakfast table, draped with antique cutwork linen, is set in place at one end of the garden room. Belying the elegant look, serviceable, child-resistant vinylized cotton covers the chairs.

Diversions overhead, however, are handsomely counterbalanced by diversions underfoot. Foregoing investment-quality Aubussons or Savonneries, the designer commissioned New Orleans artist Merri Pruett to copy patterns from surrounding fabrics and wallpaper onto natural and painted sisal rugs. Sealed with multiple coats of polyurethane, the rugs are pretty yet childproof.

Today, the mistress of the house spends happy hours arranging fresh-cut bouquets for every room of her home. She frames her children's artwork in Lucite boxes and stands them next to antique jardinieres, their clay bowls next to Chinese porcelain fruits. She has an eye for the elegant, the time for things that matter, and a setting that testifies to both.

GIRLS' BEDROOM

Despite the pristine appearance of the little girls' room, crisp linens on the custom-carved daybeds are practical additions that can be tossed in the washer at a moment's notice.

MASTER BEDROOM

A penchant for detail is revealed in the subtle handling of the master bedroom's draperies and bed linens. The effect is rich and light — the perfect backdrop for the Louis XV-style bed, handcarved by New Orleans craftsman Fred Kempf.

3

INSPIRED BY THE PAST

By recognizing and replicating examples
of our architectural ancestry, homage is paid to the past,
and the finest examples of design
are perpetuated. And, although each period in history
sees things in its own way, there are styles that transcend
both time and the whims of fashion.
These are structures and motifs that manifest
continuity and serve as inspiration for the
designs of the future.

Loggia from Acadian
Heritage, *page* 96.

LIVING ROOM

Shades of melon and blue, taken from colors in the antique Serapi rug in the living room, are repeated in the draperies and Rhode Island wing chairs. A rare tray-topped Queen Anne tea table is positioned in front of the Philadelphia Chippendale sofa. The secretary is attributed to Benjamin Frothingham, 1734-1809, renowned cabinetmaker, Revolutionary War soldier, and friend of George Washington.

A CONTINUUM OF TRADITION

Collecting American antiques and works of art is a way of life for a Franklin, Tennessee, couple. Soon after they married and acquired their first home, they began accumulating Americana — a pleasurable pastime which has proved a wise investment.

Through the years, they have assembled five different collections. Two they gave as dowries to their daughters, thereby forming a nucleus for each young woman's growing interest in American antiques. Another, consisting of early Tennessee and other Southern furniture made of native cherry and walnut, is still intact at their summer home near Franklin. Unfortunately, perhaps the most important grouping, consisting mainly of Philadelphia Chippendale furniture, including fine examples by renowned cabinetmaker James Gillingham, was lost when fire destroyed the couple's first home, a 1793 log house.

A fifth collection of eighteenth-century American antiques is the couple's current passion. So great is their devotion to the period that they have duplicated the historic Dwight-Barnard house in Deerfield, Massachusetts, for their home. A dignified gambrel-roofed saltbox stained dark brown

DETAIL
A niche framed with classic molding creates a decorative focal point in the living room.

and trimmed in pink, it is an ideal backdrop for the distinguished furniture it holds, all selected on the basis of outstanding craftsmanship and design.

Becoming a recognized expert in the field of American antiques takes years of dedicated research. More than textbook knowledge, it requires seeing, touching, and examining objects to determine their credentials. Because of his hands-on expertise in Americana, the respected homeowner/collector was asked to head the Tennessee Executive Residence Preservation Foundation, an organization working diligently to acquire documented pieces for the state's official residence. His approach toward these acquisitions is methodical, and he fervently believes that by studying each item and learning its background, new insight of the period in which it was made is gained.

KITCHEN

The "keeping room" is the scene for authentic open-fire culinary fare. The New England walk-in fireplace is fitted with an eighteenth-century trammel to raise and lower pots over the flames. Two continuous-arm Windsor chairs flank the maple Queen Anne tea table, which is set with antique pewter.

Working with young collectors also brings great personal satisfaction. He encourages them to invest in fine pieces of furniture that will establish the taste level of their home. To investors of all ages, he recommends buying top-notch handcrafted reproductions. Not only are they reasonably priced, they are certain to be the antiques of tomorrow.

The couple's personal domicile is imbued with a sense of the eighteenth century. In the parlor, tea is served from delicate porcelain tea sets and is accompanied by cakes and cookies made from old recipes. Beds are made with antique linens trimmed with handmade tatting and lace and are warmed by old jacquard coverlets. So complete is their infatuation with the period that they often forsake modern appliances and cook over an open fire in a "keeping room" lined with authentic cooking utensils. Within this peaceful yet energetic setting is found a true appreciation for a way of life that transcends the passage of time.

MASTER BEDROOM

A Rhode Island canopy bed is adorned with an early nineteenth-century jacquard quilt. In front of the window, a miniature Queen Anne desk sits atop a Pembroke table.

DINING ROOM

The handsome 1720 Connecticut architectural cupboard of pumpkin pine has a carved tree-of-life motif at the base of the deep shell and a rosette on the keystone. A set of Philadelphia Chippendale chairs surrounds the New York State Federal pedestal table. Eighteenth-century wine rinsers and matching Matthew Bolton candelabra and epergne complete the setting.

LIVING ROOM

Handhewn cypress beams salvaged from the French Opera House in New Orleans and walls upholstered in cotton brocade emphasize the gracious dimensions of the large living room. A painting by Richard Clague and others by artist W. A. Walker hang above the sofa. The open armchair is Régence, circa 1720. The walnut chest, oak clock, and beechwood buffet are eighteenth-century French pieces.

ACADIAN HERITAGE

The fortunes of war have much to do with the tenor of a people's history — and in some instances, the pitch of their rooflines as well.

In 1702, when the French and English began warring over North America, the Acadians (French colonists who had established the Canadian settlement of Acadia in the early seventeenth century) fell into disfavor with the British king because of their Francophile sympathies. Forced into exile, many of the Acadians migrated south into what was then the French territory of Louisiana. They brought with them building traditions from medieval France — simple, boxy structures that had taken on sharply peaked roofs designed to shed the snows of Canada.

These early dwellings were built of heavy timber framing covered with wide horizontal boards and stood on wooden sills placed directly on the ground. Later, when brick became available, it was used to fill in the spaces in the timber framework of the walls, resulting in a superior structure and

EXTERIOR

The brick walls of this cottage were covered with plaster to seal the brick against the elements. Louisiana rockers and eighteenth-century olive jars set an inviting mood.

providing insulation against extreme weather. Because summers in southern Louisiana are long, hot, and humid, the houses were fashioned with high ceilings to allow the warm air to rise and the cooler air to settle. Still later, galleries appeared. These covered areas provided shade from the sizzling sun and the luxury of leaving the windows open during rainy periods. Houses on these lines were built along the Louisiana bayous by Acadian descendants, who became known as Cajuns.

Because this Cajun cottage measures eight thousand square feet, it might seem a contradiction in terms. But because its architect, A. Hays Town of Baton Rouge, empathizes with the spirit of the old Cajun residences, the new house fits easily and naturally into that genre.

MASTER BEDROOM

Walls in the master bedroom are upholstered in fabric and complemented by a mixture of prints used for the handquilted bedspread and on the love seat and chairs. The walnut bed was designed by the owner and built by David Pruett of Natchez. Handmade needlepoint pillows add a personal touch to the love seat, which sits atop an antique Serapi rug.

DRESSING ROOM

A dramatic print covers the walls of the dressing room. The delicate porcelain basin and fittings add appealing contrast to the room's exotic look.

DINING ROOM

(Overleaf) An eighteenth-century Dutch brass chandelier and a fruitwood bahut à deux corps exude a quaint charm in keeping with the mood of the dining room.

The original structure was built as a first section in 1962. Additions made in 1970 and 1981 to accommodate a growing family were designed to look like more Cajun houses surrounding a quadrangle. They are connected by airy loggias, and each addition is as prominent as the original so that an interesting traditional facade is presented from all sides.

On the interior, some liberties have been taken with tradition by combining old-world architectural accents with a collection of Country French antiques, a profusion of Oriental rugs, and a rich array of cotton and linen prints on the walls and furniture. The scale of the furnishings is crucial to the decor of the rooms, and in each, designer Dan Bouligny has employed a mixture of natural fabrics that boosts the rustic appeal of exposed ceiling beams, old brick, and wide-board wooden floors.

No doubt the early Acadian settlers would be surprised to see how their idea for a simple dwelling has grown. But just as surely, they would feel quite at ease in the cozy atmosphere of this up-to-date Cajun cottage.

DEN

A custom rug, designed by Dan Bouligny and adapted from designs in the owners' collection of American Indian pots and baskets, offers brilliance of color on a subdued ground.

CLASSIC & ENDURING

ENTRY

The Chinese fretwork design of the stairway in the entrance hall was copied from a staircase in Bohemia Manor in Cecil County, Maryland. A family portrait hangs above a shield-back settee, and a pair of Derby vases rests on an Adam console with a serpentine front. The English Georgian mirror is flanked by a pair of Georgian sconces. The rug is an antique Serapi.

EXTERIOR

A grove of tall pines shelters The Knoll, an imposing brick residence in Columbia, South Carolina, designed by architect Edward Vason Jones and inspired by Virginia's Woodlawn Plantation.

Like its inspirational ancestor, Virginia's Woodlawn Plantation, this imposing house stands solid and dignified, the epitome of an eighteenth-century American house of European descent. Yet for all its old-world charm and characteristics, it dates back only a little beyond two decades. Situated by one of the numerous small lakes around Columbia, South Carolina, it would be at ease beside its peers along the Potomac.

Such a grand house was not originally considered for the site. The couple, who had small children at the time, envisioned a simple Carolina Low-Country design with a veranda across the back overlooking the lake. This changed when their architect, the late Edward Vason Jones, saw the property, which is all but surrounded by water. This persuasive gentleman felt so strongly that the setting called for a formal structure that they bowed to his judgment and for the most part followed his recommendations.

Everyone agreed that to achieve the desired patina, old

materials must be used. Agreeing was the easy part, but locating the components was difficult. First, handmade oversize bricks from the demolished Columbia Female College built in approximately 1856 were found for the exterior. Then heart pine flooring from an 1860 house and finally cornices and wainscoting from a razed Charleston, South Carolina, building were purchased. All materials were stored in a warehouse until the time when enough had been assembled to begin construction. When that day arrived, skilled craftsmen were called in to assemble the pieces and, where necessary, to recreate missing ones.

Building a formal house proved to be a decision that complemented the homeowners' life-styles: both are involved in the decorative arts, she as an interior decorator and he as the owner of a noted antiques store. As they travel in England and America buying for clients and the shop, they are able to acquire a number of choice pieces for their home.

MASTER BEDROOM

A Portuguese needlepoint rug contributes restful colors in the master bedroom. The gesso mantel and pilasters came from a Charleston home built in the early 1880s.

LIBRARY

The colors in the library's Portuguese needlepoint rug blend harmoniously with a Sheraton-style satinwood chair, which has its original needlepoint upholstery. Prints by J. F. Herring, Sr., hang above the Sheraton-style sofa.

DINING ROOM

An obi serves as a runner for a Sheraton-style pedestal table decorated with antique porcelain geese, Sheffield candelabra, and an English silver-and-crystal centerpiece. Chippendale-style chairs add a graceful touch to the dining area, and a Portuguese needlepoint rug adorns the heart pine floor.

Formal design and rare antiques notwithstanding, both were adamant that no room should be "off limits" — the house was to be enjoyed from basement to attic. No area reflects this attitude more completely than the entrance hall: with doorways opening to the front and back, it is the center of activity. Early on, bicycles and dollhouses shared space beneath the decorative fretwork of the staircase. As time rolled along, toys made way for supper parties, then for dances, and finally for wedding festivities. At Christmas, a twelve-foot tree, decorated with cherished ornaments, traditionally holds the place of honor.

Classic and enduring in its pastoral setting, this home borrows architectural inspiration from the past, but has its roots firmly planted in the present.

LIBRARY

Marjorie Hinman Craft sculpted the bronze bust that is situated behind a painted Regency chair in the library.

LE PETIT CHANTECAILLE

Standing majestically on the east brow of Lookout Mountain, commanding a view of Chattanooga and the Tennessee river below, is an exquisite French *manoir*. Perfectly proportioned and authentically detailed, it is the work of the late James Means, an architect whose designs are distinguished by their strong association with the past.

The house was built for a lady with both emotional and ancestral ties to France that include her grandfather Jean Félix Brizzie, who received the *Médaille Militaire* from Napoleon III. It was not surprising, then, that when she first saw the Château Chantecaille in Touraine, a region in central France, she decided to copy it, *en petit,* for herself.

To accomplish the task, she solicited the talented Means, whose reputation for designs espousing spaciousness, high ceilings, and splendid moldings was well known. She knew him to be a devotee of the style of elegant, classical home she admired.

FOYER

Rare Dufour handblocked panels were fitted to the curved niches at either end of the foyer. An antique marble paneled floor contributes to the grandeur of the reception area. The marbles used for the floor were cut to order in Italy and shipped to Chattanooga, where they were assembled like a giant jigsaw puzzle.

GARDEN

Viewed from the drawing room balcony, the flower garden resembles the configuration of a Persian carpet. In the background is a magnificent vista of the Tennessee mountains.

The approach to the house is down a straight drive lined with maple trees and ending with a forecourt paved with cobblestones. Built of old, handmade bricks acquired when an antebellum building in Chattanooga was razed, the home is the epitome of graceful architectural symmetry, its balance accentuated by twin chimneys and two *oeil-de-boeuf* windows that form dormers in the roof.

Part of the reception area, just inside the front door, is a long foyer with an antique marble mosaic floor. Siena, cipolin, verd antique, and rouge royal marbles used for the floor were cut to order in Italy and shipped to Chattanooga, where they were assembled on the site like a giant jigsaw puzzle. *Demi-lune* alcoves at either end of the room are lined with rare 1820 Dufour handblocked watercolor panels depicting the travels of the Greek hero Telemachus.

The interior was planned by David Richmond Byers III to complement the drawing room walls, which are finished in

KITCHEN

A collection of blue-and-white transfer earthenware is displayed on the stove hood in the kitchen. The arms of an old brass billiard lamp were turned up to form the unusual chandelier.

DRAWING ROOM

Silk brocade in a ribbon stripe covers a pair of beechwood fauteuils. Over the rare blue-and-white Saint Anne marble mantel is an exquisite trumeau which was part of the original boiserie. The lampas used on the Louis XVI sofa was inspired by a fragment of fabric designed by the renowned eighteenth-century Lyons designer Philippe de La Salle.

period Louis XVI paneling. The panels were carefully removed from a Parisian town house and restored and recomposed for the Chattanooga residence. The celadon paint of the panels, as well as the turquoise and cerulean blue moldings, are intact.

Decorated with a warm palette of colors, each room has its own strength and character. The handsome library, with walls of olive green felt, functions as a music and television room, while the dining room, resplendent with fine English antiques, is the scene of more formal affairs.

Taken as a whole, this small château with its authentic detailing and sensitive balance is a masterpiece of fine design intended as a celebration of the *joie de vivre.*

HALLWAY

An unusual overdoor treatment was created by using frames handcarved by the late H. Millard of Atlanta to fit portraits of an eighteenth-century gentleman and his wife. An antique gilt mirror hangs over an elaborately carved French Provincial bombé commode. Custom-designed rugs complement the French blue woodwork.

MASTER BEDROOM

In the master bedroom, the owner adapted the look of Napoleon's tented bedroom. The walls are covered in black-and-white striped cotton ticking. The carpet is a fine copy of an old Aubusson.

4

BREAKAWAY PLACES

To get away from it all!
Reason enough for a place devoted
solely to the pursuit of enjoyment and amusement.
A special spot — be it seaside or
countryside — where laughter and fun are the
order of the day. If pleasure means solace,
a quiet place. If pleasure is people,
a busy place. Rituals and traditions
can be packed along or sent packing —
whatever it takes to entice,
to make one happy.

Loggia from Paradise
Found, *page 140.*

LIBRARY

*An easy, relaxed assemblage of
furniture and memorabilia contributes
to the restful atmosphere enjoyed in the
home's inviting library.*

SOLITUDE IN THE COUNTRY

Thriving on the seasonal crush of tourists and the episodic changing of the political guard, Washington, D. C., radiates an aura of power and energy. The electricity that makes it an exciting place to live, however, also makes it a place from which its residents occasionally like to get away. That is why interior designer Sam Morrow spent six months searching for a small house in the Middleburg area of Virginia.

What he finally found did not seem promising. Well on its way to ruin, the farmhouse had been abandoned for seven or eight years. The windows gaped vacantly, and there were no doors, no wiring, and no plumbing. It was, in fact, no more than two little log houses, adjacent to each other, in the middle of a cornfield.

Although it had always been the home of simple working people, the house possessed the prestige of a long history. The middle section, now the central hall, was built in the late 1700s. In the nineteenth century, a plain log storage room was added to one end. After the Civil War, another two-story

EXTERIOR

When the owner found this farmstead near Middleburg, Virginia, the house was a near ruin in the middle of a cornfield.

house was built at the other end, but not attached to the original structure.

The designer was determined to reclaim the house and to update it with every possible modern convenience. In the center section, partitions were torn out to create a single large room, and a door was added to serve as the main entrance. The small, narrow windows were replaced with ones twice as long to admit more light and provide pleasing proportions. The massive stone fireplace was original to the house, but a mantel, which had been a ridgepole in one of the barns on the property, was added.

The Victorian addition, now the library, boasted a bay window. This was balanced with a matching window on the other side of the room so that each framed a splendid view of gardens, fields, and rolling hills. The two unattached structures were linked, and the space between them was used to accommodate pipes and wiring.

HALL

Painted in the style of seventeenth-century English artist John Wootton, a portrait of a whippet dominates one end of the hall. Below it, the Queen Anne sideboard displays a collection of eighteenth-century South American silver. Although the metal is luxurious, the workmanship is rough, giving these pieces a special affinity for country furniture.

LIVING ROOM

(Overleaf) The oldest part of the house doubles as dining room and informal sitting area. Chairs upholstered in subtle tones blend unobtrusively into the stonework of the massive fireplace, giving center stage to the nineteenth-century kilim rug and sixteenth-century English dining table. A supply of reading material is always handy in the seventeenth-century English barrel, which was turned from a single piece of elm. Tall turned candlesticks are also seventeenth-century English.

KITCHEN

Kitchen cupboards and paneling are pine, recycled from the partitions that originally subdivided the rooms into even smaller living quarters. Above the early nineteenth-century spindle-back chair hang still-life paintings, the subjects of which the owner thought fitting for the room.

Furnishing the house was simply a matter of moving the contents of the owner's beach apartment in Delaware to his new home. A trim man of dignified bearing, he came into interior design by first dealing in antiques. Over the years, he has assembled a handsome collection of English, French, and Early American pieces. Mostly oak, they offer a country spirit appropriate to the setting. And they mix with an uncalculated grace, reflecting their owner's sense of beauty and design.

The move to the country now requires that the designer commute one hour each way to and from his office in Washington. It is a price he is more than willing to pay. Living in surroundings that are consistently pleasing, remote from the rest of the world, has a splendidly restorative effect. It is the best of both worlds: having the luxury of isolation when you want it, without the danger of becoming a hermit.

BEDROOM

Crafted in France in the late 1600s, the canopy bed and night table were simple country interpretations of the Louis XIII style.

MAIN HOUSE LIVING ROOM

Art objects on display in the spacious living room of the main house range from fine arts and crafts to ancient artifacts. Many of the shells exhibited on the mirrored shelves were found on St. Simons, Sea Island, and Cumberland Island. Artist Comer Jennings executed the paintings of shells on the Mexican colonial table, and the magnificently carved and painted blue heron is by Frank Shields.

LIVING SEASIDE

St. Simons is one of the most alluring of Georgia's Golden Isles, a chain of coastal islands which, over the years, has proved irresistible to pirates, preachers, poets, and patriots. These lush, subtropical bits of land remain as inviting today as they were in 1717, when Sir Robert Montgomery, an English real-estate entrepreneur, envisioned the development of a string of feudal baronies along the shore and described the area to prospects as "our future Eden." Unquestionably, Sir Robert's predictions were a bit overenthusiastic and his timing off by a few hundred years, but there are many people today who swear by the islands' Edenic qualities.

A substantial part of St. Simons's charm lies in its residences. Historically, homeowners living on St. Simons have enjoyed unrestricted freedom of expression; until recently, for instance, there was no development plan. What evolved then was a village with houses and cottages, large and small, standing side by side. Encouraged by the free-design climate, many of those who built on the island exercised great

POOL

Topiary ligustrum and colorful portulaca in terra-cotta pots flank doors leading to the screened porch of the guest house. Confederate jasmine is used to soften the wall behind a small garden.

Main House Living room

Three large polished turtle shells from the Cayman Islands complement artist Ben Smith's line drawing above the sectional sofa and chairs in the main house living room.

Entrance Walk

Lush trees and plants overhang double doors that lead from a gracious walkway to the entrance of the main house, one of two cottages that form a single residence on St. Simons Island.

Living Room

Sea colors on the walls and ceiling brighten up the guest house. Large wicker sofas and colorful, patterned rugs invite beachcombers to relax and enjoy the holiday spirit. The plant-filled cachepot decorated with swaying palm trees is by Norman Schulman. The painting on the dining room wall is by S. Garlington.

ingenuity in construction — ingenuity, in this case, exemplified by a breakaway house where, unfettered by codes and circumstances, two cottages were joined to make one.

Originally, the two small frame cottages had been built on property owned by the same family. Such unpretentious houses, with exposed block foundations, were typical of those found on St. Simons, many of them constructed by people of nearby Brunswick who came to the beach to escape the city's heat. Later on, one of the two summer homes was enlarged and remodeled as a permanent residence, and a pool was added. The smaller house was used for guests until the present owner devised an ingenious way to link it to the main residence. The properties are now unified by an eye-filling outdoor area: the pool, a garden, a wooden walkway, and an enormous screened porch which was added to the smaller guest cottage. A putty color on the exterior and surrounding walls of both houses helps to unite the two. Inside, however, each has a distinctive personality.

The larger, sophisticated Mediterranean-style house has muted taupe tones on walls and upholstered pieces, providing a backdrop for collections that range from sculpture, paintings, and ceramics to bone and shell fossils. The smaller cottage is decorated with a sense of humor. Walls, ceilings, and floors are a riot of bright sea greens and blues. Furniture is predominantly wicker, with pastel-colored cotton rugs scattered about for relaxed, easy living.

MASTER BEDROOM

An elevated platform in the master bedroom provides an extraordinary view of the ocean. Marguerite Stix executed the shell graphics which hang below an antique fish trap on the wall.

GUEST BEDROOM

Museum posters in simple metal frames accent the brightly colored walls of the guest bedroom. On the bed are blue polished-cotton pillows and a handstitched blue-and-white quilt.

In this holiday atmosphere, life revolves around the pool and the porch during much of the year. These are by no means the only attractions, however. At high tide, a scant one hundred feet from the front windows of the main house, sailboats, shrimp boats, and barges glide past, an ever-changing parade at sea. And nature provides her own "sound and light shows," from glorious sunrises and sunsets to spectacular electrical storms over Georgia's Golden Isles.

KITCHEN

Seafood specialties are ready for cooking in the kitchen of the main house. A wooden bowl turned by Ed Moulthrop rests on the countertop. The painting of seagulls is by Ben Shute.

THE TAJ-GARAGE

The moment of truth for the owner of a rambling vacation home in the North Carolina mountains came when she realized that her children and a growing troop of grandchildren were gradually taking over. Like the swallows coming back to Capistrano, they returned each summer in ever-increasing numbers. And so like a good mom (and also to preserve her sanity), she decided to leave the nest to them and find a less hectic summer place for herself.

Not wanting to be completely isolated from all the vacation hoopla, she hit upon the idea of taking an existing three-car garage on the edge of the property and turning it into her own private vacation retreat. There, she would be within shouting distance of her brood, but far enough away for peace and quiet. With this thought in mind, she rang up

LIVING ROOM

At the kitchen end of the great room, a Palladian-style window looks out on lush mountain greenery. Atop the custom-designed rug, which depicts wild flowers native to North Carolina, casual seating provides a place for conversation and also offers a vantage point for admiring the spectacular panorama.

WALKWAY

Behind the converted garage vestibule, a covered walkway leads to the new structure, which is topped with a squirrel weather vane.

Charlotte, North Carolina, friend and architect, Jim Meyer, to get his ideas. He came right over, and they plotted and soon agreed on a wrinkle that only two nimble minds could devise: the garage would serve as a "front," a sort of trompe l'oeil entry to an entirely new structure.

The design is a tease; a surprise; an astonishment. The tattered old garage remains much as it has always been: secluded, almost invisible, a given that shields the new structure from the eyes of an established community resistant to drastic change. But while two of the openings into the garage remain for use by automobiles, the third has been transformed into an entrance foyer where flowered wallpaper, a bench, a hat rack, and a multicolored rag rug offer a welcome to unsuspecting visitors. At the rear of the garage/foyer, double doors open upon the surprise: a covered bridge with white railings curving above laurel and rhododendron and leading to a brand-new, barn red building with sparkling white trim.

ENTRY

A sprightly wallpaper and colorful rag rug strike a welcome note in the remodeled entry hall, formerly a portion of the existing garage.

PORCH

The porch offers a breathtaking view of the Blue Ridge Mountains. A decorative porcelain rabbit centerpiece adds a light touch to the outdoor furniture grouping.

BEDROOM

Muted shades of peach and blue make for a restful bedroom. The floral fabric on the bedspread and chaise adds to the feeling of homey comfort.

Poised on the edge of a precipice, the house has a steeply pitched roof and large plate-glass windows that offer a marvelous vista of the North Carolina countryside. Open decks wrapped in the same white railings provide an optimum view. To the rear of the house are the living room/dining room/kitchen and master bedroom suite, all located on the main floor. This large space seems to have the capability to expand or contract depending on the size of a gathering and is gracious rather than cavernous. A bushy-tailed squirrel, woven into the carpet, entices guests to follow his lead down a winding staircase to three guest rooms.

The influence of mountain flora and fauna is repeated in accents throughout the house. The living room rug, designed by the owner, is a mosaic of wild flowers indigenous to the state. Lamps, lampshades, tablecloth, and even bathroom tiles suggest the trailing fuchsia plant that grows to such perfection in the cool mountain climate.

Princes and princesses have been among those teased and surprised by this delightful place. And they have been served hot biscuits and country ham alongside untitled gentry who are made to feel like royalty by the wit and charm of the maharani of the Taj-Garage.

LIVING ROOM

The graciously proportioned living room features French doors that open to the ocean beyond. A colorful print fabric of purple, pink, and moss green flowers and vines adds a colorful accent to the neutral tones of the room.

PARADISE FOUND

Could this be the house people had raved about, the one designed by premier Palm Beach architect John L. Volk? The couple from Tennessee registered disbelief when they first saw the house.

But when the agent unlocked the door and they stepped into the spacious entrance hall with its eleven-foot ceiling, they gasped. Before them stretched a columned loggia overlooking a keyhole-shaped pool, and behind the loggia, they could see a living room with fanlight-crowned French doors opening onto vistas of the Atlantic Ocean.

The rooms were cool and serene, with generous space and light. The series of columns and arches on the loggia set up a rhythmical symmetry for rooms that opened to the outside. This house, with the sea curling nearby, was the epitome of unpretentious seclusion in the best Florida tradition.

Members of the eastern establishment, Midwesterners, and a few Southerners — such names as Du Pont, Mellon, Ford, and Scranton — have been coming to Jupiter Island, Florida, for years, just as their fathers and grandfathers before them. The island is not a resort, but rather a deep-rooted community with the studied, low-key atmosphere of a New England summer club. Library, theater, church, the Yacht

ENTRANCE

Pink geraniums growing in profusion in plain white planter boxes add a gentle complement to the simple exterior of this Florida residence designed by Palm Beach architect John L. Volk.

Club, and the private Jupiter Island Club contribute to its stability. In 1961, a zoning ordinance restricting a certain residential area to single-family dwellings was challenged and upheld. The circuit court judge wrote that a counterpart for the community "cannot be found elsewhere. . . . The Town doesn't want what many others have, but many others would be better off if they had more of what this Town has and wants to keep — seclusion, solitude, and tranquility."

Here where the speed limit does not exceed thirty miles per hour, coconut palms, plumbago, hibiscus, raccoons, foxes, even wildcats, it is said, flourish in the lush climate. Stretches of dense, tropical foliage are interrupted by tiny beach cottages and magnificent mansions with lengthy approaches through mangrove thickets.

SITTING ROOM

Simple rattan furnishings in the poolside sitting room reflect the laid-back informality that prevails throughout the interior of the house.

DEN

The dark tone of the glossy walls in the den offers a quiet respite from the brilliant Florida sunshine.

Few houses on the island are "decorated" in the strict sense of the word, and this one is no exception. The simple, informal furnishings were not even purchased explicitly for this house, and the neutral color scheme, splashed with lavender, peach, and moss green accents, was selected long ago. More emphasis is placed on comfort than on elegance here. It is a holiday house where the bottom line is easy living, and in this case, easy means fun and pretty, too.

The plan of the U-shaped residence is as practical as it is unorthodox. The entrance and flanking guest bedrooms comprise the front one-story wing. The gallery beyond, backed by the kitchen, constitutes the closed end of the U. Not visible from the front, a rear two-story wing on the ocean side houses the living room, dining room, den, and master bedroom above. The arrangement of the bedrooms affords owners and guests not only privacy and access to the pool but also a magnificent view of the Gulf Stream's navy blue currents.

Always beckoning is the beach, a tempting stretch of sand that lies just a stone's throw away. Occasionally, when the weather turns sullen and the Atlantic's cascading thunder roars, the sounds seem an intrusion in this paradisiacal barrier island where a calm and peaceful silence prevails.

5

CONNOISSEURS' COLLECTIONS

*Fate has decreed that all
inveterate collectors must be incurable; that once
set upon a course, they will pursue the
object of their desire with the vigor of a crusader.
Intrinsic worth shall not be at issue. It
is the chase that motivates, becomes the driving
passion, and constitutes the
spirited adventure.*

Gallery from Blending
Styles Boldly,
page 164.

LIVING ROOM

Once covered in seven layers of paint, the stripped pine walls of the living room now form a handsome backdrop for artwork. A wooden boat made in Haiti and a curved cylindrical ceramic piece by Bill Farrell are prominently displayed on the coffee table.

OUT OF THE ORDINARY

If Victorian gingerbread embodies the stereotypical notion of a Key West residence, then this house breaks the mold. With its dramatic reduction of extraneous lines and its refined spatial relationships, the house is a singular expression in a neighborhood known for its exuberant character.

Built before the turn of the century, the house was a Bahamian-style structure with an interior hallway that opened onto a succession of rooms. Originally, a bathtub and pump were located outside. By 1920, it had gained two upstairs spigots, but no hot water. One spigot was for rainwater, the other for well water.

Although a Key West family lived in the house for many years, it was unoccupied when the current owners bought it in 1981 and embarked on the restoration project that was to last for two years. For openers, there were many aspects of the place that were not pleasing to one of the new owner's artistic sense of balance. These had to be changed. She knew what

EXTERIOR

Lush, tropical vegetation enhances the appearance of a nearly one-hundred-year-old restored Key West residence.

149

she wanted to achieve, but because for her form comes before function, instituting these ideas posed a problem. To help find solutions, she appealed to architect Robin Bosco.

Of prime importance was the staircase. It was completely boxed in, and she wanted it to be freestanding. To achieve this effect, it was necessary to tear out the confining walls, replace the old stairs, and reinforce them with steel. Great care was taken to duplicate the original newel post, railing, and spindles. Together, the owner and architect worked out ways to expand existing doorways, enlarge windows, and remove the walls and ceiling in the dining room to expose old pine beams in the A-frame construction.

Architectural designer Steven Justi was also involved in the redesign of the house. By keeping interior detailing to a minimum, he contributed to the successful reshaping of the interiors into a showcase for the owner/artist's many collections of antiques, fine art, and accent pieces.

Then came the problem of the paint. Seven layers applied to the walls over the years had to be chemically removed. From battleship gray to yellow, blue, pink, and white, each layer required a special chemical to remove the different type

DINING AREA

One of the owner's own painted vessels stands on a pedestal beside the reconstructed floating staircase. On the dining table are Costa Rican folk art toys. Shelves along the wall contain pre-Columbian artifacts, European glass, and ceramics by American artists such as Peter Voulkof, Beatrice Wood, and Paul Soldner.

WORKROOM

(Overleaf) The sunny workroom is filled with whimsical objects and personal treasures, such as a collection of wooden boxes and primitive toys from Central America. Photographs of artists, scholars, and family members contribute to the warm atmosphere. The large ceramic pot is an early work by the homeowner/artist.

of paint. Now, unpainted pine walls crown the interior with their own textural richness and form a handsome background for art.

Fabrics, used sparingly, and furniture, chosen for line and form above function, are an integral part of the scene. Two linen-draped chairs in the living room appear sculptural. The polished coffee table serves more as a display surface for a carved Haitian primitive and a ceramic piece by Bill Farrell than its original purpose. And the dining room table, though functional, showcases an arrangement of Costa Rican folk art and toys. Something unusual, something crafted, something intimate is found everywhere.

The artist, who is a serious collector of pre-Columbian, Native American, and African art, is recognized for her three-dimensional constructions. Her works have been widely exhibited and are now part of permanent collections in America and Europe.

Although travel is a necessity, it is here in the free climate of this artist's haven that she likes to work. Having completed the instant project, she moves on, leaving behind the one-hundred-year-old house now transformed into a highly visible expression of her personal art.

BEDROOM

An unexpected flourish of color dominates the bedroom. A mixed-media work by Robert Rauschenberg and a primitive painting by Haitian artist Tebo flank the window.

LIVING ROOM

*Wallcovering applied square by square and lacquered conveys the effect of
leather-covered walls in the downstairs living room. Chippendale mirrors and rare
Chippendale chests flank the custom-made mantel, which is decorated with a
Chippendale chinoiserie clock, Colonial ivory orbs, and eighteenth-century ivory
carved-and-turned candlesticks.*

A SOPHISTICATED APPROACH

In an age when space travel is commonplace and biofeedback is a household word, the term "good vibes" to describe an exciting, creative experience is readily understood and accepted. It is also a good way to explain the successful collaboration between an internationally recognized designer and his client on the latter's Washington, D. C., town house. Although the two had worked together on three previous projects, this, the fourth, was their masterpiece.

It was the designer's penchant for strong, masculine decor that first attracted the client's interest. Both are drawn to colors resembling fine wines, fabrics that bring the tactile pleasure of velvet and suede, and objects that are bold and heroic in scale.

A second shared enthusiasm is the acquiring of fine antiques. While working on the first house, the designer suggested that the addition of a few choice pieces would add depth to the scheme. Soon, one man's vocation became the other's avocation, a pleasurable discipline that has taken him to important auctions and antiques houses around the world in his quest for museum-quality treasures.

In the instant case, the designer became interpreter rather

EXTERIOR

The gracious Georgian facade of this Washington, D. C., town house presents an elegant setting for the collection of treasures arranged within.

than director. His role was to act as a sounding board for his client's ideas, problems, and desires. He then carefully collated the input and translated it into reality.

It fell to the client to act as director. Having amassed one of the most important collections of English antiques in the country, his knowledge is respected and his advice sought by museum directors and antiques aficionados alike. Clearly, the collection was to be the star of his new domicile.

The client owned a pair of colossal Chippendale mirrors, and the ceilings of the new home were not high enough to accommodate them. To solve this dilemma, major structural changes were necessary. So the ceiling was raised and the floor lowered on the first level, creating ample clearance for the beautiful mirrors. But this in turn reduced the ceiling height on the second floor, now housing the newly relocated kitchen and dining room. To disguise the low ceiling required pulling out all the design stops.

SECOND FLOOR SITTING ROOM

A late seventeenth- or early eighteenth-century Coromandel screen serves as a backdrop for this view of the upstairs parlor. Chippendale torchères display a pair of mid-eighteenth-century candelabra. A sang-de-boeuf Chinese vase rests on the gold leaf Chippendale table. A rare lacquered fretwork Chippendale chair is placed beside a late eighteenth-century English table.

DINING ROOM

A painting by Brazilian artist Manoel Fernandes stands out against the Bordeaux red wool selected for the dining room walls. The Chippendale table is set with English crystal, circa 1710, nineteenth-century Davenport bone china, and Queen Anne glass candelabra. A classical mid-eighteenth-century mirror hangs above a late eighteenth-century English chest. Shelves display Chinese import china.

MASTER BEDROOM

*In the regal master bedroom where
exquisite antique pieces prevail, the
undisputed pièce de résistance of the
collection is the museum-quality
Regency table that serves as a desk.*

ENTRY

*At the entrance to this Washington,
D. C., town house, an
eighteenth-century English candlestick
rests on a rare English Regency
credenza. Original Piranesi prints are
from a collection entitled* Monuments
of Rome. *Mid-eighteenth-century side
chairs display their original English
tapestry upholstery.*

Lighting was recessed, molding and trim were painted chalk white, and walls were covered in a deep Bordeaux red wool. Parquet floors were left bare to create the illusion of blending with the furniture and to minimize awareness of the low ceiling. The effect is at once dramatic and romantic — ideal for dining.

Designing to please rather than impress required blending contemporary wallcoverings, rugs, and fabrics, as well as furniture, with the outstanding period pieces. The result: a winning production where good vibes stimulate the visual pace and create an image of rich comfort.

LIBRARY

A mid-eighteenth-century classical mirror attributed to Inigo Jones is a dominant feature in the inviting library. Rich colors found in the drapery and upholstery fabric add warmth. Mid-eighteenth-century chairs flank the fireplace, and Italian Renaissance horses rest on the late eighteenth-century mantel. Above it, a Chippendale frame sets off a chinoiserie painting on glass.

BLENDING STYLES BOLDLY

The proof, as they say, is in the pudding. And for those raised on a more traditional diet of seventeenth- and eighteenth-century American furnishings and antiques, the exceptional and delectably presented American Empire fare used throughout this San Antonio, Texas, house is cause to stop . . . and savor a closer look.

Part of a well-manicured five-acre estate in one of the city's most beautiful historical districts, the house started life as a ranch in the 1880s, a time when its views stretched across the corrals and hill country of a horse farm on the outskirts of Victorian-era San Antonio. The main residence was remodeled in the 1920s to reflect its present sunny Mediterranean styling and dimensions.

But every generation has its preferences and priorities. Today, the home's informal villalike facade belies interiors expertly fashioned to evoke the grace and ambience of an English manor. Rooms brought to life with fool-the-eye artistry and classic embellishments serve as the perfect foil for a fine-tuned mix of American Empire period furnishings and a superlative assemblage of modern art.

ENTRY HALL

Classic embellishment was created by master trompe l'oeil artist Richard Neas in the entry hall of this San Antonio residence.

EXTERIOR

Once a ranch house on the outskirts of Victorian-era San Antonio, this inviting residence was remodeled in the 1920s. The original house dates from the 1880s.

BACK HALL

Richard Neas painted the walls and woodwork of the back hall leading off the gallery and sun porch to resemble a gaily striped, tented pavilion.

Because the homeowner is intensely involved in the arts on a personal level, as well as being recognized as a driving force behind several local and national organizations, the interior demanded rooms with a strong "public" presence. The result is an admitted gallerylike atmosphere, which remains compatible in terms of overall design philosophy with other, more private portions of the house.

One of the beauties of this philosophy is the use of an exuberant array of contemporary artwork as an ever-changing backdrop for an impressive collection of American Empire furnishings. The integration of these two interests, though initially unexpected, is on reflection not at all surprising, as both are distinctive statements of their time.

The American Empire style, which began in 1810, was fashioned by native-born craftsmen during what many people consider the most exciting period of our national history,

ENTRY HALL

The deftly colored faux marbre floors and woodwork set a purposefully formal theme, underscored by a pair of méridiennes by Quervelle, circa 1820.

GALLERY

(Overleaf) The doorway from the gallery to the dining room separates works by Larry Bell at left and Karl Knaphs at right. To the left of the mahogany table is an Earl Staley oil.

corresponding with the first great territorial expansion and migration westward. Taken together, both collections gain: one representative of the best of selective modernity, the other indicative of a clear-sighted "Lone Star" hindsight.

Setting the stage for the enjoyment of these portable treasures is the intricate architectural ornamentation provided throughout the home by artist Richard Neas. Elaborately stained floors and deftly fashioned faux finishes in the entrance hall, as well as the whimsical, painted rear hall, attest to his superb creativity.

Such interior decoration and the collections showcased provide an expansive range of personal choices within traditional limits — a charming cultural oasis for celebrating the pleasures of individuality.

GALLERY

An arched doorway frames a view of the gallery. Hanging above the carved Philadelphia mantel, circa 1810, is a 1936 abstract by H. Bowden.

SUN PORCH

The sun porch sparkles with a blue-and-white color scheme set by the cobalt hue of the waxed concrete floor, scored and painted to resemble tile. Fabrics were selected to enhance the collection of blue-and-white porcelain.

FOR ART'S SAKE

A palpable sense of space irradiates this penthouse condominium in a luxurious Houston high rise far above the city. The two-story windows of the living room look out onto a vast terrace and the wide Texas sky. Clusters of skyscrapers soar within the sweep of the horizon, shining citadels by day, walls of shimmering light by night.

The owner of the 5,200-square-foot unit purchased it as a shell. A bachelor at the time, he wanted a spectacular setting to house his burgeoning collection of primitive art. But before the ink had dried on the contract, he became engaged. And with an eye toward the future, his wife-to-be introduced him to interior decorator Billy Francis.

Together, this energetic and unabashed booster of the Lone Star State and his artistic fiancée presented the designer with their basic requirements: an architectural arena that would showcase the collection, comfortable surroundings emphasizing Texas materials and furnishings, and — need it be said? — a dash of the elegant.

Of course, the challenge, as well as the chance to coordinate the nuts-and-bolts construction of the floor space with the landscaping of the enormous terrace, was eagerly accepted by the designer. And while the building's angular configuration dictated a plan that offered a limited number of walls on which to hang paintings, these limitations presented a rare opportunity to reform the interior within the architectural givens.

GALLERY

An African shield, carved wooden figures from New Guinea and Africa, a Haitian mask, and a Chinese coolie hat are showcased opposite a painting by Walter McCown in the gallery.

Today, the dynamic results begin just inside the entrance. The staircase, itself a work of art, softens the structural angles, and in poetic showdown with the massive upholstered pieces and the fireplace, it establishes a necessary light touch in the main living area. Furnishings from the owners' former homes provide contrasting forms with which to work. Biedermeier accents combined with nubby wool upholstery fabrics, smooth leather, and sleek mohair serve to soften the masculine feel of the quarters. Texas clay and mesquite floors, pecan cabinetry and millwork, and tables of native fossil stone anchor the condominium solidly to the region.

The simple elegance of the decor directs attention to the many primitive masks, shields, bowls, totems, carved figures, and fine prints displayed with fearless panache throughout the apartment. Natural-tone kilim rugs complement the collection, and at night spotlights dramatically play up textures and contours like torchlights in a dusky glade.

But it is the apartment's own real-life parkland, the

LIVING ROOM

The fireplace, designed by interior decorator Billy Francis, divides the living room into two seating areas.

BEDROOM SITTING AREA

In the sitting area, a raised fireplace is set within a marble wall. A painting by Stanley Boxer hangs above the Biedermeier sofa.

A Bösendorfer Imperial grand piano stands at the foot of a sweeping free-form suspended plaster-and-steel staircase in this two-story penthouse condominium located in downtown Houston, Texas. Rich carpeting on the stairs and landing contributes warmth and texture to the Texas clay floor. Various primitive figures and artifacts and a painting by Walter McCown are visible on the second-floor gallery.

two-level terrace constituting a veritable backyard atop the building, that is one of the home's most extraordinary features. Colorful and hardy plants able to withstand Houston's simmering sun and searing winds are staples here, as well as a ceremonial fishing canoe seemingly moored in a state of suspended animation.

The vessel, which the owners found on a small island off Taiwan, was shipped across the mountains to Taipei, then across the Pacific to Houston, where steeplejacks hoisted it up the face of the building to the top floor. It now rests in splendor, a striking focal point silhouetted against the sky.

LIBRARY

Rich pecan paneling and shelving add warmth to the library, which houses a collection of pre-Columbian art, books, and memorabilia. The Biedermeier sofa is upholstered in black horsehair.

ART & ARTISTRY

This artist's Colonial-style house is unlike anyone else's. It may appear quite conventional from the outside, but one has only to cross the threshold to realize the difference. It is there; it is recognizable; it is undeniable. More than a house, it is a vehicle for the showcasing of her work and a private repository for a collection of works by other artists as well.

The entry, painted a lively shade of pumpkin, sets the tone. Two of the artist's sculptures stand on either side of a French Provincial love seat upon which are placed an intricately decorated pair of dolls, primitive works from Puebla, Mexico. On a pedestal in the corner is a sculpture by Niki De Saint-Phalle, and hanging on the stairwell wall is a drawing by Jesse Poimboeuf. In total contrast to these artworks, an elaborate chandelier purchased by the homeowners in Venice provides an element of surprise — a touch of unexpected refinement in a highly individual arrangement.

The house is decorated with Spartan simplicity. There are no draperies at the windows. Wide-slat venetian blinds

ENTRY

Beneath a Venetian chandelier, two of the artist's sculptures flank the French Provincial love seat, which holds a pair of dolls from Puebla, Mexico. A sculpture by Niki De Saint-Phalle rests on the pedestal in the corner, and the drawing on the stairwell wall is by Jesse Poimboeuf.

perform the function of adjusting light. Furniture is minimal. In the living room, a small sofa, a wicker chair, an occasional table or cube comprise the sum total. Walls in the living and dining rooms are stark white, a ploy to give precedence to the artwork hanging on them or positioned against them. An eccentric array of objects, collected with an eclectic's eye, are artistically arranged on tabletops. Artifacts wired for light provide illumination, and rugs, handwoven by artisans from a small village near Madrid, are clearly works of art.

A major portion of the collection, which in variety might rival that of a small museum, contains both modern and primitive objects. The den, painted brilliant emerald green with white trim, exhibits pre-Columbian, African, and American Indian treasures. Here the glass-top coffee table, made from the axle of an old vegetable wagon found in Palermo, Italy, holds an American Indian bowl, ceremonial

LIVING ROOM

Papier-mâché horses from Guadalajara guard Hans Hofmann's gouaches, while a Cameroon mask is poised to join a visitor on the black Mexican cane-bottom couch.

LIVING ROOM

A six-foot painting is the focal point of interest in the living room. It contrasts with the African, Spanish, Egyptian, and Mexican art objects displayed above the corner secretary and an antique santo statue from Mexico. A Yoruban footstool rests in front of a rattan chair.

DINING ROOM

What the owners call "trash and treasures" are displayed in a glass showcase in a corner of the dining room. The major painting above the case is by Charles Blank.

figures, and a windmill made by a ninety-five-year-old folk artist. Above the mantel is one of the artist's own gesso-and-enamel Styrofoam cutouts on canvas entitled *Boogie Woogie with Apologies to Mondrian*, while two Indian polychrome wooden musicians flank a basket of wooden Indian rasps on the hearth.

Although at this point in time the artist could rest on the reputation of her canvases, she is not content to be idle. And while her work has progressed through many stages, she has always maintained a fiercely independent and personal style, which is clearly evident in her home's distinctive decor.

DEN

Pre-Columbian treasures and African statues fill the shelves in the den. The curio case in the center is filled with a collection of smaller pre-Columbian, African, and American Indian artifacts. At the base of the fireplace, two Indian polychrome wooden musicians stand at attention, with a bowl of wooden Indian rasps between them. For the position of interest over the fireplace mantel, the owner selected her own gesso-and-enamel Styrofoam cutouts on canvas.

6
CONTINENTAL TOUCH

*The imprint of the Continental style has
been woven into the fiber of our domestic architecture
and our interior design as well.
Houses that could be lifted straight from the English
countryside, the boulevards of Paris,
or an estate in Italy grace towns and cities across
the nation. Admired for their sense of
order and quality, these structures attest to an
uncommon way of life. Their romantic
influence presents a tangible tie to the elegance of
old-world grace.*

SMALL COMPASS

The business of making other people's houses attractive takes imagination — and much more. It demands extraordinary taste, tact, and a full measure of self-confidence. Personifying all the aforementioned attributes is Joe McKinnon, a soft-spoken, modest man whose artfully crafted interior designs enliven some of the most beautiful and imaginative houses in his resident city, Birmingham, Alabama. Fearless when mixing and matching colors and patterns, he readily admits to a penchant for red, a soupçon he considers necessary to every successful design scheme.

True to this conviction, he has reached the pinnacle of the exuberant style for which he is noted within the small compass of his very own home. Once an unexceptional bungalow, it has been transformed into a delectable miniature Italianate villa.

LIVING ROOM

An air of sumptuousness prevails in the living room, which is dominated by an overmantel mirror and plasterwork from an English manor house. The fireplace, with mirrored walls on either side, is flanked by French iron sconces, a pair of Louis XVI chairs, and Italian consoles. The Portuguese rug repeats the pattern of the fabric on the walls. A sparkling Louis XV chandelier features topaz fruits.

EXTERIOR

Ivy, boxwood, and hanging baskets soften the house's facade, and the painted exterior wall trim enhances the European ambience.

ENTRANCE HALL

A richly patterned fabric covers the walls of the entrance hall. Leather knife boxes rest on the Louis XVI table, and a Directoire mirror hangs above. An Italian painted canvas screen and a Louis XV cabinet displaying a terra-cotta bust heighten interest in the corner.

When he and his wife bought the house, extensive remodeling was required to adapt it to their taste. It had problems, but it also had exceptionally high ceilings, and there was a plausible way to expand and rework spaces without disturbing the integrity of the building. The front door was moved from the center to one end of the house, thus creating space for an entrance hall. What was once a narrow solarium became the dining room, and a garden room and balcony were cantilevered out over the back garden. Arches were also installed to divide the rooms and reinforce an old-world feeling.

Inspired by impressions garnered from numerous trips to Europe, the designer let his imagination run free. Colors and designs chosen for the painted exterior were borrowed from

MASTER BEDROOM

A nineteenth-century Korean screen provides a center of interest in the master bedroom. Bedcoverings of contemporary geometric fabric act as a calm background for the riot of pattern on needlepoint pillows. A luxurious Louis XV chandelier illuminates the scene.

GARDEN ROOM

The garden room extends across the back of the house from the master bedroom to the kitchen. Trellises covering the skylights and Spanish tile flooring promote a garden look. French iron containers add a decorative touch.

the Tuscany region of Italy, while the formal plan of the entrance and parterre was inspired by gardens in France.

Despite the small scale of the house, a sensation of spaciousness prevails. Employing the technique known as overscaling, the designer filled the rooms to capacity with grand furnishings and accessories. Bold fabrics of varied colors and rich textures cover walls, floors, and pieces of large furniture. The decor, enriched by subtle lighting, is reflected in strategically placed mirrors that further enhance the illusion of space and carry the light from room to room.

Such diffusion of textures and hues is not for the faint of heart. It is a unique formula devised by the sure, unwavering eye of a design chemist. Here, the alchemy works, revealing the delicate balance between what is expected and total surprise.

DINING ROOM

In the long, narrow dining room, a topaz Louis XV chandelier, resplendent with grapes, pears, and apples, hangs above a custom-made French parquetry table decorated with a floral arrangement in a nineteenth-century French birdcage. Louis XV chairs are covered in red or green needlepoint.

Dining Room

An oil painting by Arthur Weeks and the shimmering iridescent hues of the linen window treatment echo colors of the cottage cutting garden beyond the dining room doors. Eighteenth-century Dutch chairs slipcovered in hyacinth blue surround the glass dining table.

A COUNTRY FRENCH RESIDENCE

A cobbled courtyard and stucco walls rising to high gables distinguish this beautifully crafted twenty-year-old Country French residence located in a suburban pocket of Atlanta, Georgia. Enriched with architectural bits and pieces from local landmarks, the house has provided the perfect setting for a family's enjoyment. In and of itself, this is quite enough. But for this home's owner, it has been this and more.

Her story begins some years back when, as a child, she enjoyed leafing through her mother's magazines. On one occasion, she remembers being fascinated by an article depicting an accomplished Parisian lady shown at home in the beautifully decorated rooms of her manor and yet — true to the French tradition — totally at ease in surroundings that were comfortable and livable as well. The pictures made a deep impression on the young psyche, and years later when she stepped through the front door of this house, those

REAR LAWN

Masses of blooming begonias edge the rear lawn, while an old window, imaginatively recycled from a home in France, makes a charming garden gate.

MASTER BEDROOM

French lace provides a delicate counterpoint to the massive lines of an oak headboard fashioned from an antique Portuguese church bench. An Italian reproduction Adam-style settee and tea table invite an early morning or late evening repast.

memorable scenes flashed through her mind. Without question, she knew at once that the house should be hers.

Traditional, yet individualistic, bounded by colorful arbors and intimate walled cottage gardens, the house radiates a European sensibility reminiscent of dwellings seen in the French countryside. By recognizing and building upon this appealing old-world integrity, the owner has placed the mark of her own decorating taste and style on the home's interior furnishings. But while it is her touch that is most impressive, she is quick to give the original owners credit for the almost palpable aura of antiquity built into every nook and cranny.

Constructed in 1965, the house's authentic design evolved from an inspired collaboration between the original owners and architect/builder J. S. Garrison. The result is a special home environment — a thoroughly practical, modern residence that has its design roots firmly planted in the past.

Delightful aspects of this creative vision at work can be

FAMILY ROOM

The family sitting room reveals a rich blend of European furnishings and accessories. Comfortable seating is arranged around the fireplace. Paintings hanging above the fireplace mantel are by Dorothy Gay Poole.

seen in architectural details that utilize structural elements imaginatively recycled from older homes and historic properties in the surrounding area. The bricks used as flooring throughout much of the main level, for instance, were originally part of sidewalks in nearby Decatur, Georgia; leaded casement windows came from the solarium of the Robert Maddox estate, now the site of the Georgia governor's mansion; the heavy beams supporting the ceiling in the family sitting room are from an old engine house; and the tongue-and-groove pine floor used in the dining room was found in an old house in Marietta, Georgia. The pièce-de-résistance cobblestones — used with such remarkable effect in the front drive and courtyard area — were rescued in the nick of time from streets about to be paved over during construction of the Atlanta Stadium parking lot.

Less tangible, perhaps, but just as important is the very

SITTING ROOM

A Staffordshire dog collection is displayed in the sitting room beneath a Venetian canal scene painted by Antony Vorauer.

SALON

Assembled on the soft-toned Portuguese needlepoint rug in the salon are a period Louis XVI sofa and Louis XVI side chairs. In the foreground is a Louis XV bergère upholstered in plaid silk.

special design philosophy that governed the planning and building stages of the house and that remains very much in evidence today. It is decidedly Country French, but not to the exclusion of other styles and periods. With the help of Atlanta designer Nancy Green, fine seventeenth- and eighteenth-century French Provincial antiques, interspersed with less formal pieces and colorful accessories, are reminders of European influences.

In this luxuriant setting, where light from tall terrace doors falls on the soft impressionistic colors of the decor, there is no break with the grace of the home's good French style. Instead, there is a look that seems to say, *c'est fini . . .* beautifully finished, indeed!

MASTER BEDROOM

The master bedroom sitting area is arranged around a working fireplace, which features an antique Renaissance mantelpiece. The complementary colors of the needlepoint rug and polished cotton fabric covering the chaise and dressing table chair enhance the owner's collection of blue-and-white china.

LIBRARY

A wealth of architectural detail and a Spanish-style carpet of muted tones enhance the rich ambience of the library. English artist Hugh Robson painted the oval panel above the fireplace.

A CONTINENTAL STANCE

When first glimpsed, this classical Palladian-style residence summons a vision of villas in the peaceful Italian hills of Tuscany. As in a Renaissance painting, such elements as stone arches, clipped hedges, and weather-stained statues heighten the sense of illusion. But contrary to these images, the setting for this imposing structure is near the city of Atlanta, with terraces that overlook not the Arno but the Chattahoochee River in the distance.

The long, straight drive climbs sharply toward the yellow stucco house dressed in limestone at the crest of a hillside. Here a broad paved courtyard set with bricks stretches the length of the house. Statues representing the four seasons gaze wistfully from niches that echo the curve of the central archway. The house stands paramount in its setting just as architect James Means envisioned it, for to him site selection was of primary importance.

In 1971 when the owners decided to build on this choice riverside acreage, property that had been held by their family

EXTERIOR

Architect James Means designed this Palladian-style residence in a suburb of Atlanta. A coral-colored roof of Spanish tile complements the home's yellow stucco walls.

for years, they were considering an informal, country design. But when the architect saw their collection of fine Continental furnishings, he convinced them that such a proposed farmhouse would not ultimately be to their tastes.

Construction of the elegant three-story, twelve-room house that rose in its stead took three years to complete. Midway through the process, the couple traveled to Italy, architectural plans in hand, to purchase the keystones, chimney caps, columns, statues, mantels, and other elements that contribute to the overall effect. While they spoke no Italian, and the sales representative in Vicenza from whom they bought the stone pieces knew no English, the three somehow managed to overcome the language barrier. And when the elements arrived and the stone pieces were unpacked, a crane hoisted the chimney cap and slowly lowered it onto the chimney. The dimensions were perfect: the bonnet slipped on as smoothly as silk, and the statues slid easily into their niches.

Though not large, the rooms of the house, with their eleven-foot ceilings, convey a sense of order, graciousness, and generous space. The living room, garden room, and

Garden Room

A profusion of plants luxuriates in the garden room. An antique Indian cornice section adorns the doorway, and a carved wooden Italian chandelier is suspended overhead.

LIVING ROOM

In the living room, a Portuguese needlepoint rug plays up the rich colors of custom-woven taffeta draperies trimmed with brocade. A Dutch eighteenth-century painting is displayed above a bronze by Clodion centered on the mantel. French chairs flank the fireplace, and a pair of antique bergères comprise a conversational arrangement.

DINING ROOM

A Russian chandelier illuminates an antique American dining table and an eighteenth-century English sideboard. The same draperies used in the living room are repeated here.

library on one side of the entrance hall balance the dining room, kitchen, and garage on the other. Wide moldings and quality craftsmanship, characteristic of the architect's work, engage the eye.

Rooms are decorated in subtle combinations of soft, mellow tones. Darker shades on the first floor, terra-cotta in the entrance hall, and deep yellow in the living room give way to peach on the second floor and pale pink on the third.

Each room reveals the imagination and individuality of the mistress of the house. She has assembled her furnishings with the invaluable help of Edith M. Hills, an eminent Atlanta designer who has an eye for color and a feeling for inviting, livable interiors.

Though the exterior is Palladian in flavor, the interior reflects an assured Continental approach that combines French and Italian pieces with Oriental rugs and European paintings. These furnishings, all of the finest quality, are much used and well cherished. It is a house filled with treasures accumulated over the years . . . a villa of grace and ingenuity. *E molto bello.*

MASTER BEDROOM

In the master bedroom, a Sheraton four-poster bed appears to frame an Italian chair. An antique copy of a portrait of Madame de Pompadour is displayed above the fireplace. The Oriental rug adds interesting pattern and color.

LIVING ROOM

The living room features a wallpaper scene by Joseph Dufour. The sofa, covered in rose velvet, is flanked by French eighteenth-century chairs. An antique Chinese wedding chest of painted pigskin serves as a coffee table, and a miniature eighteenth-century fruitwood chair, with a needlepoint flower appliquéd onto its silk upholstery, adds a charming touch.

A WISE FOLLY

It evokes an illusion of Paris, this superb pavilion, its wrought-iron trim, clipped hedges, and decorative finishes indicative of those found in the French capital city. But it is just that — an illusion. For despite its Gaulish air, the house is in Memphis, Tennessee, the long-cherished "dream come true" of its owner.

The brick veneer and plaster residence stands in the same intown area where the owner and her late husband lived when they first married. And although they later moved to a larger Tudor-style home where they were to reside for many years, it was always their plan to build a small, perfect French manor in the old neighborhood.

In 1966 after the husband retired from his cotton business, the couple decided the time had come to make their fantasy a reality and launched into what they lovingly referred to as their "old age folly." New Orleans architect Edward B.

PATIO

On a small patio off the master bedroom, wrought-iron garden furniture invites reading and relaxation.

Silverstein was selected as the person best qualified to articulate their wishes, the only admonishment being that the house was to be formal French in feeling and that the materials used must be of the finest quality obtainable. Armed with such enviable instructions, the exuberant architect embarked on the creative assignment of a lifetime: to design a *maison magnifique.*

During the two-year construction period while the architect continued his quest for the finest marble and wood for the interior detailing, the couple canvased the antique shops of New Orleans, Chicago, and New York, as well as major European cities, for furnishings and accessories suitable for the new house. Upon completion of the project, the three principal participants were able to congratulate themselves on a job well done.

The house is approached from wide limestone steps that lead to large, inviting double doors opening to the foyer. Here, handmade moldings and an Italian marble floor provide

POOL

A terrace at the back of the house serves as an extension of the living room and the dining room. A kneeling figure by Mexican sculptor Enrique Alferez adds a graceful accent.

MASTER BEDROOM

An Oushak carpet and a combination of salmon and cream create a feminine atmosphere in the owner's bedroom. The French Provincial bed from her childhood home in New Orleans is covered with a delicate spread crocheted by her mother. Pillows were made from dresser scarves.

ENTRY

A pair of monkeys carved from lemon wood greets visitors in the entrance hall. The monkeys, considered a symbol of good luck, were commissioned by the archbishop of Paris in 1740. Handmade moldings and a gleaming Italian marble floor provide a splendid setting for an eighteenth-century fruitwood commode, purchased in New Orleans. The trumeau above exhibits its original glass.

a splendid setting for a pair of carved lemon-wood monkeys, which preside as impudent twin majordomos over the entry.

Two sets of paneled doors lead from the entrance hall into the formal salon. Perfectly balanced between the openings is a fireplace enhanced by a delicately carved oak mantel purchased in France. In this intimate, light-filled setting, many of the unusual pieces collected by the couple are displayed.

A splendid wallpaper mural by Joseph Dufour, part of a series appropriately entitled *Monuments of Paris,* dominates the wall above the sofa. The panel was rescued from a London town house demolished during the blitz of World War II. A Chinese pigskin wedding chest, with painted figures depicting the event, is used as a coffee table. Around the room, a myriad of objects — many cast in bronze or carved in semiprecious stones — such as monkeys (a favorite motif), birds, and frogs creates a charming bestiary of tiny animals. Each of the figures, artistically arranged on tabletops, was chosen for the delight of the collectors rather than as planned accessories, creating a surprisingly harmonious potpourri that brings a note of individuality to the room.

Doors opening into the dining room provide a continuation of the open, airy ambience of the adjoining salon. Oval-back chairs covered in brilliant apricot cut velvet offer a stunning contrast to oyster white walls and the exquisite French grisaille painting above the marble-topped commode. French doors in both the salon and dining room open onto a slate terrace that extends across the entire back of the house and overlooks the pool and gardens.

During the ensuing years, the house has gone beyond the owner's prerequisite requirements for formality and elegance. With time it has gained the rich patina of warmth and enjoyment . . . the essence that makes a house a home.

DINING ROOM

Oyster white walls provide a perfect foil for rich apricot and gold colors in the dining room. An old Italian terra-cotta urn placed on the commode complements a French grisaille painting, which is flanked by Russian sconces. The rug is an antique Oushak.

7

TIMELESS TRADITION

*Houses with a past . . . . those
American originals reclaimed from deterioration,
or possibly demolition, and infused with
new life to stand as testament to the
residential architecture of other ages. Rescued by
a unique breed of historian — those who
enjoy the laborious task of chipping
away the ruin inflicted by
time to uncover the resplendent
original — such restorations enlighten us
to the importance of
our heritage.*

Gallery from Rooms
with a View, *page 238.*

RESURRECTED & RESPLENDENT

Extraordinary efforts were made to preserve the Dr. David Ross house. Local citizens wanted it to remain where it was built about 1749 beside the northern branch of the Potomac River in Bladensburg, Maryland; but no buyer willing to restore the down-at-the-heels historic property stepped forward. So when a lumber company bought and planned to replace it with a lumberyard, a local builder dismantled the historic house brick by brick.

The bricks, numbering forty-three thousand, along with doors, windows, flooring, paneling, and handmade nails, lay piled in a garage for the next four years. The splendid jerkinhead pent-roofed Tidewater mansion, documented as having been built by a surgeon in the Continental army and used to shelter wounded soldiers during the War of 1812, seemed consigned to twentieth-century oblivion.

By extreme good fortune, however, a prominent Maryland businessman had just secured a tract of land in the Western Run Valley of Baltimore County, where he and his wife intended to build. He commissioned Bryden B. Hyde, a

ENTRY

The handsome closed-string staircase with walnut newels and balusters in the front hall was inspired by the staircase in the Magruder house in Bladensburg, Maryland. Welcoming flowers top a Chippendale lowboy made in Philadelphia between 1730 and 1770.

EXTERIOR

The back of the residence incorporates the front facade of the Ross house to take advantage of an incomparable prospect of Maryland hunt country. Telescoping out from the main block of the 1749 Ross house are the two sections of the new wing. Modernization includes a large reflecting pool, two small lily ponds, and a hillside cascade that aerates and cools the water before it reaches the pools.

Baltimore-based architect specializing in Colonial restoration, to design a house after the fashion of the English colonists. But Hyde, an officer for the Society for the Preservation of Maryland Antiquities, an organization that had tried to save the Ross house, suggested that rather than a replication, they should consider rebuilding an authentic old house. The owners' immediate and positive reaction to the mountain of wood and bricks was characteristic of the man whose dynamic leadership was to galvanize the Maryland Historic Society to innovative achievements a decade later.

Drawings, measurements, and photographs taken before dismantling the house, along with records from the Historic American Building Survey in the Library of Congress, comprised the documents for rebuilding. And after great quantities of earth were moved to nestle the foundation of the house into the hillside, the materials were transported, and construction from ground to third floor began.

A new wing was incorporated on the east with bricks saved by reducing the eighteen-inch-thick walls of the original house to brick with concrete block backing. Crushed oyster shells, sold commercially for chicken feed, were added to the mortar of the new walls to achieve the oyster shell hallmark of Tidewater authenticity. And new pine, purchased for exterior porches and beams, was sandblasted to simulate two hundred years of weathering.

PARLOR

Included in original paneling around the parlor fireplace are balancing closets. A semicircular cupboard with scalloped shelves displays nineteenth-century Staffordshire, eighteenth-century Whieldon, and Prince William of Orange creamware, circa 1755. A pair of English Queen Anne mahogany chairs with serpentine top rails and stiles flanks the fireplace.

BREAKFAST ROOM

Adjoining the kitchen, this spacious room was fashioned exclusively from the beams and siding of an old New England building in order to maintain continuity throughout the house. The walnut cupboard was made in Pennsylvania in the eighteenth century. The painted Windsor braced-back armchairs are favorite pieces, enjoyed for their lightness and indestructibility.

In the course of the two-year project, the owners' interest in Colonial America took them to Winterthur and Williamsburg to study restoration; to Connecticut where, in one weekend, they located eighty-seven suitable old doors for the house; and to antique dealers up and down the East Coast for the appropriate furnishings.

As it stands today, not a detail of the house looks out of character, from the period H-L hinges and lift latches on the doors to the blown glass of the windowpanes. Layers of paint stripped from the walls of the old house revealed original pigments, and most of the wood trim has been repainted in like tones. Because eighteenth-century ambience is preferred to the effects created by electric lighting concealed behind

LADY'S BEDROOM

The lady's bedroom contains a Sheraton pine and maple tester bed, a family heirloom. Adorning the bed is a pieced Drunkard's Path quilt, probably made in Virginia around 1860.

KITCHEN

In the kitchen, a modern oven is concealed behind the old oven door of the fireplace. Instant hot water, an icemaker, and a warming oven are all effectively disguised, while antique apparatuses are prominently displayed. Dangling from the fireplace mantel are some of a collection of five hundred antique devices whose uses are now obsolete. The dome-shaped device on the counter is an eighteenth-century lignum vitae oyster shucker.

DINING ROOM

The present-day dining room contains an original Ross house catercorner fireplace and surround and a built-in corner cupboard taken from a mid-eighteenth-century house on Maryland's lower eastern shore. A prized collection of over one hundred pieces of Prince William of Orange creamware is prominently displayed in the corner cupboard. Four unmatched Queen Anne walnut armchairs and side chairs grace the Virginia Queen Anne mahogany drop-leaf table.

window cornices and in the ceiling, candles, purchased by the gross, light chandeliers in the living areas.

Though having stipulated initially that the rebuilt house was to be a comfortable home, not a museum, the owners are quick to admit the debt of gratitude owed for the knowledge and expertise gained through this remarkable endeavor. Their newfound commitment to recapturing the glories of eighteenth-century design has converted them to purists devoted to perpetuating and sharing the past. A sweet debt indeed.

LIVING ROOM

A colorful print chintz at the windows and on the Chippendale-style sofa and chairs harmonizes with the Herez rug. A lacquered box used as a coffee table was designed by Keith Knost and hand decorated in Hong Kong. Its color complements the salmon hue of the damask fabric on the wing chair. A portrait of a young woman is painted on a wooden panel, circa 1830.

THE HOUSE ON PRINCESS STREET

In 1762, when Thomas Shepherd obtained a charter for the town now known as Shepherdstown, West Virginia, he called it Mecklenburg. It was then just a village in the Commonwealth of Virginia, with a growing population of German and English settlers. In 1798, the town was renamed in honor of its founder, whose descendants still live there, and then midway through the Civil War, it became part of the new state that was created out of the Old Dominion.

Shepherdstown, however, has no identity crisis. Well situated on the Potomac River, it is a town of small businesses and shops, a lively society, and informed citizens who cherish the town's past and are intent on preserving its history. Little more than an hour's drive from Washington, D. C., and in easy reach of historical landmarks and recreational diversions, the town is a pleasant place to live — "a well-kept secret," whispers an inhabitant in a confidential tone.

EXTERIOR

Constructed around 1793, this Federal-style house in Shepherdstown, West Virginia, is typical of those built for merchants and tradesmen during that period.

For all these reasons and for some he calls "ineffable," interior designer Keith Knost decided to settle here in 1973, a move he has never regretted. He became active in the Historic Shepherdstown Commission, a group determined to preserve the buildings in the heart of town. One of his new friends had lived in her family's home on Princess Street for over sixty years. A visit to her house, filled with local memorabilia from two centuries past, was a treat for him. The friend, in turn, realizing that the newcomer was genuinely interested in the town and its welfare, decided that he would be the right person to succeed her as owner. And in 1980, Knost found himself proprietor of the house, known locally as the Chapline-Shenton house for the families who had first occupied it.

The property was deeded to William Chapline on April 12, 1793, for twenty-two pounds, and the house, similar in design to others nearby, was built shortly afterward. Designed in the prevailing Federal-style of the time, it is small in scale and strongly Adamesque in its symmetry and classic decorative elements.

Inside, the house had such fine features as high ceilings, an open winding stairway to the attic, a fireplace in every room,

ENTRANCE

Delicately scrolled risers and simply turned spindles on the staircase serve as a backdrop for the fine antique porcelains and table in the entrance hall.

DINING ROOM

Philadelphia chairs with inlaid backs, a Virginia banquet table, and a West Virginia corner cabinet in the dining room all date from the early nineteenth century.

and deep windowsills. In place were the original "cross and Bible" doors with strap hinges and some remnants of the original handblown window glass. Still, the task of restoration and renovation proved monumental.

Every room had to be replastered, and the bathrooms, products of the early twentieth century, had to be completely redone. Floors that had withstood multiple coats of brown paint emerged from stripping and sanding in pristine condition — if slightly warped by time.

No feature original to the house was removed. When bookcases were added to the upstairs library, existing chair rails were retained. And when the kitchen was modernized, the old fireplace was incorporated into the new design.

Although the renovation was a painstaking and time-consuming process, it was the actual furnishing and

DINING AREA

An eighteenth-century Pennsylvania table is set for an informal supper. The chairs are early nineteenth-century Pennsylvania antiques. Terra-cotta pottery on the mantel and a copper teakettle, all by nineteenth-century local artisans, harmonize with the antique woodblocks and a collection of baskets.

redecorating of the interior that posed the greatest challenge. Extreme care had to be taken to avoid creating an atmosphere too overwhelming or grand for the modest scale of the house without sacrificing elegant surroundings. The solution was to keep the decoration faithful to the style of the Federal period while enriching the overall setting with fine furniture and fabrics.

Paying homage to both past and present, the designer chose a copy of an eighteenth-century French paper, replete with birds and flowers, to cover the walls in the entrance and up the winding stair to the top floor. Well aware that such an elegant detail would only have been found in the finest houses of the day, he thumbed his nose at convention. Perhaps it is too splendid for the simple little house . . . but she certainly wears it well.

LIBRARY

Replete with fine books and rare prints, the small library is alive with color and interest. Prints by Edward Beyer and an original Currier and Ives print grace the walls.

BEDROOM

Prints of Queen Victoria and her children, from Vanity Fair *issues of the period, testify to the owner's keen interest in British memorabilia. Printed chintz covers an antique mahogany bed made in New York around 1800.*

Parlor

The parlor features an original wraparound mantel and transom. A Russian Empire chandelier illuminates the room, and additional lighting is provided by bronze nineteenth-century French candelabra on the mantel. A painting by the Mexican artist Arivalo hangs above the fireplace. French chairs and a Sarouk carpet define the seating area. Above the card table is a painting by George Dureau.

NEW ORLEANS FLAIR

In its own inimitable fashion, New Orleans's famous French Quarter has traditionally blended the commercial with the residential, and many merchants live, quite practically, above their places of business. But like the numerous courtyards and gardens in the city which are hidden from public view, these intriguing upstairs residences are seldom glimpsed by the passing parade of visitors. Above the well-known Cafe Sbisa in the historic Sbisa building on Decatur Street is an apartment that is a classic example of such a delightful and sensible arrangement.

Because Decatur Street parallels the Mississippi River, this area was the hub of a bustling shipping port in the nineteenth century. Old records, dated 1820, show that the building originally housed a store dealing in naval supplies. Then the

EXTERIOR

The facade of the historic Sbisa building on Decatur Street in New Orleans's French Quarter gives no hint that it houses an antique-filled apartment.

233

Sbisa family, for whom the building is named, opened a restaurant on the street level in 1899 and operated it successfully until 1977, when they sold the property.

The new owners wanted to recapture the charm of the original cafe during the time when Decatur Street was the shipping and financial heart of New Orleans. They decided to expand the restaurant to the second floor and to create a convenient apartment on the third floor and in the attic. The idea was not only efficient but feasible due to a winding exterior stairway on the courtyard side of the building that provided a private entrance to the living quarters.

The apartment on the third level contains a library, music room, parlor, dining room, and kitchen. French doors from the music room and library open onto a balcony that overlooks the Mississippi River and the French Market.

The owners inherited several choice architectural features. The music room, for example, exhibits a wraparound mantel that is original to the house, and the large parlor has a similar mantel, as well as two handsome, original transoms. In the cheerful country kitchen at the rear of the quarters, a fanlight looks out on the rooftops of the famed French Quarter. As a

Dining Room

A nineteenth-century Russian chandelier provides soft lighting for the dining room. Queen Anne side chairs, upholstered in red leather, and Chippendale armchairs surround the Sheraton dining table, which has been set for a special occasion.

bonus, this level is designed so that it can serve as an adjunct to the cafe for entertaining on special occasions. The attic contains the sleeping quarters, which include two bedrooms and two baths.

The warm, eclectic interior reflects the owners' interests in a wide range of styles and periods of furniture and accessories. Queen Anne, Chippendale, and Sheraton pieces mix happily with lithographs and paintings by contemporary artists. The restoration, which required two years to complete, is now resplendent in full nineteenth-century glory.

MUSIC ROOM

In the music room, a wraparound mantel and a medallion above the wooden eighteenth-century Dutch chandelier are original to the house. Ebony and bronze Directoire candelabra flank the nineteenth-century French mirror over the mantel. The cane bergère dates from the nineteenth century.

KITCHEN

A large window in the kitchen overlooks the courtyard and the rooftops of the French Quarter. A Victorian hutch holds numerous cookbooks, and period Thonet bentwood chairs complement the fruitwood Louis XV table.

ROOMS WITH A VIEW

A garden terrace large enough for a croquet court was just one of the amenities acquired by Baltimore, Maryland, interior designer Alexander Baer with the purchase of a condominium in the elegantly converted mansion of the old Devon Hill estate. Because his former Victorian town house had required formal, traditional furnishings and constant landscaping upkeep, he opted for the easy-living alternative presented by this new space: a fabulous view, use of the grounds without the care, proximity to the city, and the opportunity to turn his talents to creating the perfect contemporary design for living and entertaining.

However, while fashioning an updated remodeling scheme for the condominium, complete with mirrored walls and ebony-stained floors, the designer began to have reservations about relinquishing the character and warmth of traditional things. Somewhat to Baer's surprise, soon after his newly devised rooms were finished he realized that "interesting to look at and easy to live in" was not his personal style. Slowly,

LIVING/DINING ROOM

Originally designed as a second-floor sleeping porch, the large living/dining room retains an open, airy aspect. A pair of chaise longues is upholstered in Italian cotton. Two Roman bronzes stand on a contemporary cigarette table. A painting, one of a pair of 150-year-old copies of originals from an English manor house, hangs above a Regency console.

EXTERIOR

Terraced gardens landscaped by Frederick Law Olmsted distinguish the view from a second-floor condominium in Devon House. The 1880s Queen Anne shingle-style mansion was built in Baltimore on the Devon Hill estate.

favorite old pieces came out of storage where they had languished, and to his gratification, the initial structural modernization of the rooms accommodated the treasured traditional furnishings beautifully.

The designer had been one of the first people to see Devon House prior to its condominium conversion. Walking through the Queen Anne shingle-style mansion, built in the 1880s, he had admired the richly paneled interiors of its twenty-five rooms. But he was not tempted to picture himself a resident until he climbed the stairs to the second floor,

HALLWAY

A painting by Robert Motherwell adorns the hallway of this condominium in a historic Baltimore mansion.

HALLWAY

Five layers of paint, lacquer, and glaze were needed to achieve the oxblood hue of the walls in the hallway. The color accentuates the gilt and jewel tones of an English Regency pier table and Chinese export porcelain.

traversed some bedrooms, and took a turn around the twenty-by-forty-foot screened sleeping porch at the west end of the house. Here, the aerielike porch, which overlooked terraces landscaped by Frederick Law Olmsted when the house was built, caught and held his attention.

With the approval from the developer and project manager, Baer revised the existing architectural plan for the porch and several connecting rooms to his own specifications. Most of the screened portions of the structure were replaced with glass and the interior architectural detailing kept simple to preserve the porch's openness. Installation of mirrors along the wall opposite the windows further emphasized the room's breadth, setting the stage for the condominium's initial sleek design.

There was probably no specific point at which Baer's hankering for traditional surroundings usurped his original contemporary plan. Using some of his old furnishings as

KITCHEN

Painted a brilliant turquoise, the contemporary galley-style kitchen is designed for convenience. The window provides a walk-up view of the magnificent gardens.

DINING ROOM

Low-voltage lighting and black surfaces create dazzling, jewellike reflections in the spacious living/dining room. Contemporary black lacquer Louis XVI fauteuils are covered in plaid taffeta and melon linen. The painting by Baltimorean Margaret Swan picks up the rose and orange hues in the antique Hamadan carpet.

BEDROOM

In the bedroom, Ken Parker's untitled lithograph, which hangs over the mantel, provides an appealing contrast to a primitive American painting of an eighteenth-century gentlewoman. The contemporary-looking yellow and turquoise vases on the mantel are actually rare eighteenth- and nineteenth-century Chinese export porcelains that the owner found in London.

stopgaps until newer pieces arrived, he saw how well they were set off by the modern design of the rooms. Gradually, more beautiful antiques were retrieved from storage. Task lighting, previously verboten in the living area so as not to obscure the view, was introduced in the form of a few lamps. Tabletops, formerly bare of clutter, accrued small collections of select objects. Having changed from unadorned windows to a minimal treatment of vertical blinds, Baer finally installed voluminous draperies of vividly striped silk moiré.

The variety of new objects and their clever arrangement was guided by a new principle: color and form, not fineness and contemporaneity, dictated compatibility. The subsequent blend of Renaissance portraits, Roman bronzes, Louis XVI fauteuils, a modern cigarette table, and eighteenth-century gilded consoles proved a feast for the eyes and an affirmation of individual style.

Seeing the glassed-in porch from one dark end of the long hallway is a surprise in this most traditional of mansion homes. But mantels, crown moldings, and other architectural detailing in most of the smaller rooms helped to make the stylistic transition a happy one. Only the kitchen survived the original concept. In the end, the designer's appreciation for the best of every age won out, and a harmonious environment that is neither strictly contemporary nor traditional prevails.

RESTRUCTURED CARRIAGE HOUSE

For three decades, a collector searched for and acquired all sorts of Americana. His collection, which ranges from good antique furniture to children's toys, burgeoned with the passing of time — so much so that he decided the time had come to create a suitable background for it.

In a San Antonio turn-of-the-century neighborhood called Laurel Heights, there stands an old Greek Revival home known as the Jarrett-Galt-Bennett House. It was designed in 1902 by the late Atlee B. Ayers, as was an adjacent carriage house. The collector chose the latter for his project, and with advice from Houston architect Joe Carroll Williams, he restructured the diminutive 30′ by 30′ building to provide not only warm and easeful living quarters for himself but also a fitting backdrop for his American nostalgia.

ENTRY HALL

In the quaint entry hall, a grandfather clock with original paint, circa 1830, towers across from an eighteenth-century Mexican bench. Over the bench is an Early American marine painting. On the stairwell wall is a framed panel of eighteenth-century American wallpaper. The balustrade is constructed of World War II tent poles found in a salvage yard.

EXTERIOR

A fine view of the exterior of the newly refurbished carriage house can be seen across the front terrace from an 1880s cotton candy booth. The terrace, paved with cast-off kiln bricks, is bordered by evergreen aspidistra.

With great care being taken not to disturb the main load-bearing walls, a slab was poured and covered with quartered Mexican Saltillo tile. Then the original nine hundred square feet, which once housed the mansion's carriages, was meticulously segmented into living areas. These included the entry, stairwell, living, dining, and kitchen spaces. The upper floor, where a hayloft had been, was converted into sleeping quarters and a sitting room. As a finishing touch, ornate windows from the 1870s were installed throughout.

On the first floor, the limited space was expanded by the addition of two terraces, one in the front and a second on the east side. The front terrace has as its focal point an 1880s

LIVING ROOM

A Ward decoy sits atop a New England slant-front maple desk. Next to an eighteenth-century maple comb-back Windsor chair, an old grain box serves as an end table.

LIVING ROOM

The living room is visually expanded by a glass wall treatment onto the east terrace, which forms a garden room. Beside a crewel-upholstered nineteenth-century wing chair is a Philadelphia dish-top table with a tripod base. The bookshelf was constructed in Boston in 1710.

DINING ROOM

The dining and kitchen areas flow together, adding to the informality of the house. Dining chairs are 1810 Sheraton with original paint. A famille rose Chinese export bowl centers the eighteenth-century hutch table. Burled bowls, antique flour bags, pewter utensils, and other bits of Americana contribute to the feeling of nostalgia.

cotton candy booth. This unusual structure cleverly doubles as a potting shed and a refreshment center for entertaining.

The living room and east terrace flow together by virtue of a glass wall framed on either side by double glass doors. This small but private terrace, accented by a bubbling Mexican fountain, is used as a greenhouse during the mild San Antonio winters. In the spring, it features ferns in hanging baskets, calendula, and, occasionally, a single white orchid. The dining room benefits spatially from its view of the front terrace through a four-section picture window and by opening directly into the fanciful kitchen.

Here, the owner demonstrates ingenuity and a considerable talent for whimsical design. Cabinets were fashioned from five-panel cypress doors, and countertops were made from the Saltillo tile used for the floors. An array of cooking paraphernalia gleaned from earlier times is arranged in a seemingly offhanded manner atop cabinets and on shelves.

Displayed within the confines of this cleverly restructured carriage house, such objects as old carousel horses, antique toy soldiers, and well-worked duck decoys glow with the intimacies of time and touch — storied reminders of a past that lives on.

RELAXED ELEGANCE

Owner: Walker Y. Ronaldson, Jr., New Orleans, Louisiana
Designer: Mary Ferry Bigelow
Photographer: John Rogers
SOUTHERN ACCENTS writer: Bonnie Warren

page 44: faux marbre wall finish created by Jeff Delude and Joanne Brigham of Mannerisms in Houston, Texas; wallpaper border by Louis W. Bowen; chandelier from the 18th-Century Shop in New Orleans

page 75: drapery fabric from Clarence House; damask sofa fabric from Bailey & Griffin; Chippendale sofa; damask armchair fabric from Scalamandré

page 76: chintz upholstery fabric from Bailey & Griffin

page 78: wallpaper from Brunschwig & Fils; wallpaper border from Schumacher; drapery and dust ruffle fabric from Lee Jofa

RHYTHM & HUES

Owner: anonymous, Mobile, Alabama
Designer: Tom R. Collum
Landscape architect: Donald Zimlich
Photographer: Gabriel Benzur
SOUTHERN ACCENTS writer: Leslie E. Benham

page 80: chair fabric from Scalamandré

page 81: club chair, ottoman, and sofa from Heirloom; floral chintz slipcover fabric from Lee Jofa; silk wing chair fabric from Terri Roses

page 82: nineteenth-century papier-mâché tray table; lit de repos cotton chintz fabric from Brunschwig & Fils; Louis XV-style lit de repos, circa 1820

page 83: sisal rugs from Rosecore handpainted by New Orleans artist Merri Pruett; slipper chair from Randolph & Hein; sofa by Heirloom; nineteenth-century Louis XVI-style wing chair; wing chair fabric from Brunschwig & Fils; Lucite table from Vivid; Régence fauteuil, circa 1725; Régence fauteuil fabric from Cowtan & Tout

page 84: wallpaper from Cowtan & Tout; Régence iron-and-marble console, circa 1725

page 85: Wedgwood stoneware; chair fabric from Brunschwig & Fils

page 86: wallpaper border, headboard and dressing table fabric from Brunschwig & Fils

page 87: chintz comforter appliqué, pillows, dust ruffle, and chaise fabric from Brunschwig & Fils

---

CHAPTER 3 INSPIRED BY THE PAST

A CONTINUUM OF TRADITION

Owners: Mr. and Mrs. Roupen Gulbenks, Franklin, Tennessee
Photographer: Paul G. Beswick

page 90: tea service from Spode

page 94: Baltimore Hepplewhite dressing table and chair; Pennsylvania Chippendale cherrywood chest

page 95: Newberry Port china from Spode; Queen Anne Stieff silverware

ACADIAN HERITAGE

Owners: Joretta and John Chance, Lafayette, Louisiana
Designer: Dan Bouligny, ASID
Architect: A. Hays Town, AIA
Photographers: Hickey-Robertson
SOUTHERN ACCENTS writer: Bethany Ewald Bultman

page 88: Louis XV bench; Charles X armchairs; armchair and bench fabric from China Seas

page 96: wall fabric from Lee Jofa; sofa from Kittinger; linen sofa and drapery upholstery fabric from Schumacher; bench fabric from Brunschwig & Fils; Régence open armchair fabric from Brunschwig & Fils

page 98: wall fabric from Bailey & Griffin; basin and fittings by Sherle Wagner

page 99: wall fabric from Scalamandré; bedspread and bed lining fabric from Brunschwig & Fils; bed designed by Joretta Chance; needlepoint pillows made by Joretta Chance; love seat fabric from Schumacher

page 100: wall fabric from Jack Valentine; drapery fabric from Scalamandré; tablecloth fabric from Bergamo; Provence refectory dining table; embroidered batiste half-curtains in the alcove from E. C. Carter

page 103: wallcovering from Kent-Bragaline; rug from Edward Fields; sofa from Henredon; chintz sofa and drapery fabric from Kravet; Yale Burge fauteuil; fauteuil fabric from Kent-Bragaline; glass-and-brass cocktail tables on faux bamboo stands from Baker; ottomans from Henredon; ottoman fabric from Stroheim & Romann

CLASSIC & ENDURING

Owner: anonymous, Columbia, South Carolina
Designer: Isola Sherrerd Hartness
Architect: Edward Vason Jones
Photographer: Van Jones Martin
SOUTHERN ACCENTS writer: Helen C. Griffith

page 106: Sheraton four-poster bed; family portrait by Robert Levers; pair of Worcester plates; French ormolu and crystal clock

page 109: Victorian crystal chandelier; Charleston Sheraton bowfront sideboard; eighteenth-century portrait of St. Cecilia; Chinese export bowl; early English decanters

LE PETIT CHANTECAILLE

Owner: Mrs. James R. Hedges, Chattanooga, Tennessee
Designers: David Richmond Byers III and Charles B. Townsend
Architect: James Means
Photographer: Paul G. Beswick
SOUTHERN ACCENTS writer: Margaret Kelley

page 110: painted Louis XVI chairs; antique Italian console and trumeau; Belgian marble pedestals

page 113: Transitional period Aubusson carpet; Louis XV bergères

page 114: coverlet fabric from Lee Jofa

page 115: custom-designed rugs from Lacey-Champion

CHAPTER 4 BREAKAWAY PLACES

SOLITUDE IN THE COUNTRY

Owner: Sam Morrow, Washington, D. C.
Designer: Sam Morrow
Photographer: Anne Gummerson
SOUTHERN ACCENTS writer: Vicki L. Ingham

page 122: chair upholstery fabric from Gretchen Bellinger

page 125: linens from Pratesi; curtain fabric from Cowtan & Tout; Louis XIII side chair upholstery fabric from Brunschwig & Fils

LIVING SEASIDE

Owners: Mr. and Mrs. J. P. Garlington, Jr., Atlanta, Georgia
Designer: Susie Garlington

CHAPTER 7 TIMELESS TRADITION

Design by
Creative Services Inc.
Atlanta, Georgia

Text composed in Centaur on
Linotron 202 by
Media Services
Birmingham, Alabama

Color separations by
Capitol Engraving Company
Nashville, Tennessee

Printed & bound by
W. A. Krueger Company
New Berlin, Wisconsin

Text sheets are Shoreweb Gloss by
Repap Enterprise Co.
Kimberly, Wisconsin

Endleaves are Curtis Flannel by
Curtis Paper Company
Newark, Delaware

Cover cloth is Payko by
The Holliston Mills
Kingsport, Tennessee